WHO'S AFRAID

OF A

HINGED-TAIL BINGBUFFER?

by

King Duncan

Seven Worlds Press
Knoxville, Tennessee

ISBN: 0-936497-02-5
Library of Congress Catalog Card Number: 87-090466

TABLE OF CONTENTS

ADDITIONS TO THIS EDITION

AFRAID OF A HINGED-TAIL BINGBUFFER

Scripture Lesson: Romans 8:15
Obejct: A blank piece of paper.

(Hold up the sheet of paper.) Does anybody recognize the animal whose picture is on this page? What? Oh, you don't see an animal? Well, you're right. I wanted to show you a picture of a Hinged-tail Bingbuffer this morning, but I couldn't find one. Maybe one of you could describe a Hinge-tail Bingbuffer for us. You can't? Well, I'm not surprised. No one's seen one of those critters for nearly 100 years. They used to tell about them in Missouri, though.

They used to say that a Hinged-tail Bingbuffer was shaped something like a hippopotamus, only considerably larger with a tail some forty feet long. It was a very slow animal, we are told, because it had very short legs. Underneath its jaws it had a huge pouch. When it wanted to catch something to eat, it simply took a rock out of its pouch with its big tail, and used its tail like a slingshot and threw the rock and hit its victim. That is why it was called a Hinged-tail Bingbuffer. At least that is what the folks in Missouri used to say.

Personally, I doubt if there ever was such a thing as a Hinged-tail Bingbuffer. I think someone's imagination got carried away with them. Imagination can do that sometimes – it can make us afraid of things that don't really exist.

Has your imagination ever made you afraid? Perhaps your imagination has made you afraid of the dark. Or maybe at school, your imagination makes you think that other people won't like you, so you become very shy. Our imagination can do things like that to us. It can make us so afraid.

God doesn't want us to be afraid. He tells people in the Bible time after time, *"Don't be afraid."* So the next time our imagination makes us afraid, let's just say to ourselves. "Aw, that's just a Hinged-tail Bingbuffer. It can't hurt me." Then let's ask God to take our fear away.

MIGHTY MOUTH

Scripture Lesson: Romans 10:5-13
Object: A tube of lipstick.

What have I got in my hands, boys and girls? It is a tube of lipstick. What in the world do you do with a tube of lipstick? Put it on your lips? Why, I don't put lipstick on my lips! Oh, I see. Girls put lipstick on their lips. Well, why do you suppose they do that? They do it to make them look pretty, don't they? Do any of you use lipstick? Well, you are a little young.

I brought a tube of lipstick with me to help us remember how important our mouths are. Can you imagine not having a mouth? You couldn't eat, could you? You couldn't talk. You couldn't kiss. That really would be awful, wouldn't it — if you couldn't kiss your boyfriend or girlfriend? Oh, I see, you're a little young for that too, aren't you?

In the book of Romans, Paul tells us that the mouth is one of the two most important parts of our body. Would you like to guess what the other part is? **(Let them guess, then read the verse.)** *"If you confess with your mouth the Lord Jesus, and believe in your heart that God raised him from the dead, you shall be saved "* (v.9).Now, what are those two important parts — the mouth and the heart. The heart believes that Jesus Christ is Lord and the mouth tells others about him. Both are important.

If we have some good news that can help other people, then we would be selfish if we didn't tell them. If Jesus is your friend, then share Him with others. They would enjoy having him for a friend, too. So the mouth is awfully important — not only to eat, not only to kiss, but also to tell others about Jesus.

HOW IS AN ELEPHANT LIKE AN AUTOMOBILE?

Scripture Lesson: Philemon 1:20
Objects: A toy elephant (or picture) and a toy car.

Boys and Girls:

Let's try a little riddle. How is an elephant like an automobile? (**Let them guess.**) That's right — they both have trunks don't they? Did you know they have something else in common? They both have radiators. Do you know where the radiator is on a car? On most cars it is in front of the fan. The radiator keeps a car's motor cool by circulating water through the motor and then back out where the fan and air can cool it.

Now where do you think an elephant's radiator is? (**Let them guess.**) An elephant is so large that it has a difficult time keeping cool. So it uses its giant ears not just as a giant fan but as a giant radiator. An elephant's ears have thousands of tiny blood vessels in them, even though the ears are as thin as paper. As the blood passes through the ears it is cooled. Then it is circulated back through the elephant. That helps keep the entire elephant cool.

Now you and I don't have giant ears like an elephant, Do we? We have to find other ways to keep cool on a hot day. We might turn on a fan or an air conditioner. We might go swimming or simply drink something cold. That's refreshing, isn't it?

Our bodies need refreshment, but our minds and souls need refreshment too. That is one reason we come to church. We have had a busy week. Maybe things haven't gone the way we hoped or planned. We've gotten tired or angry or depressed. So we come to God's house to refresh ourselves. The music reminds us of the goodness and greatness of God's love. Seeing our friends reminds us that we are part of God's family. The prayers help us re-establish contact with God. And we leave here refreshed and renewed, because we have been in the presence of God.

SPREADING OUR ROOTS

Scripture Lesson: Colossians 2:6-7
Object: A plant, complete with root.

Boys and Girls:

St. Paul writes to the Colossians: "As therefore you received Christ Jesus the Lord, so live in him rooted and built up in him and established in the faith . . . . " Here is our question today: *What does it mean to be rooted in Christ* ?

I have this plant with me today as you can see. It has leaves. What are they for? (**Let them answer.**) That is right. The leaves gather sunshine and moisture. Then there is the stem. And down here is the — what? That's right, the root. What does the root do? The root draws the plant's food and water from the soil, doesn't it? What if I were to cut off the root? The plant would have a difficult time growing, wouldn't it?

In fact, in Japan they produce tiny cherry trees — they call them dwarf trees — by cutting the tap roots on the young cherry trees. With their tap root cut, the cherry trees always remain small.

When Paul tells the Colossians to be rooted in Christ, he is telling them that we draw our spiritual growth from Christ. We don't want to be babies for ever, do we? We want to grow physically, and mentally and spiritually. So we stay rooted in Christ. We read his words in our Bibles. We pray to God in Jesus' name. We gather together with other Christian friends to encourage one another. We daily ask Christ to live in our hearts and to help us to be the people he wants us to be. As we do that we grow into healthy and mature Christians. But if we snap off this root (**snap off the root**) we stay spiritual babies. As we worship Him today, let's really spread out our roots. Let's let Him give us all the nourishment He has for us.

THE PROMISES OF GOD

Scripture Lesson: Genesis 15: 1-12, 17-18   2 L∂ C
Object: Jar of babyfood (or some other baby item) and a star (cut of
          cardboard would be fine).

I have two objects this morning, boys and girls. One is this
jar of baby food — see the happy baby on the jar. Sometimes
babies don't look that happy when they are eating baby food,
do they? Do you remember when you used to eat baby food?
That was a long time ago, wasn't it? I imagine that it doesn't
seem a long time ago to your mothers and fathers.

But what possible connection could there be between a jar
of baby food and a star? Well, our Scripture lesson tells us.
There was once a man named Abraham. God made Abraham
a promise — that he and his wife Sarah would have a baby.
Then God told Abraham to look up at the sky at all the stars
shining that night. Abraham could see thousands of stars.
God promised Abraham that one day his descendants would
be more numerous than the stars in the sky. What are descendants, boys and girls? They are your children and your children's children and then their children, etc. God promised
Abraham that one day his descendants would number more
than the stars.

Oh, that thrilled Abraham. He and Sarah wanted a child
so much. There was a problem, though. They were getting
pretty old. It would take a miracle for them to have a child.
But you know what? It happened that Abraham and Sarah
had a baby and its name was—what?   **(Let them guess.)**
Abraham and Sarah had a baby boy and named him Isaac.
They had a baby because God promised them they would— God
is always faithful to his promises. God never makes a promise
that He can't keep. God has promised us that when we are
gathered together in His name, He is here. That means that
God is in our worship service this morning. Something good is
going to happen today because God is here. God always keeps
his promises.

11

THE HARDEST LESSON TO LEARN

Scripture Lesson: I Kings 17: 8-16
Object: A little cake.

What is the hardest lesson in life to learn, boys and girls? Is it arithmetic? Is it science? I believe the hardest lesson in life to learn is to **share**.

The story in our Scripture lesson is about a widow who didn't have much in the world. All she had was a little cake — a little cake for her and her son. The prophet Elijah comes to her and asks her to share that cake with him. Oh, what a big request that was. It is one thing to share when you have a lot, but when all you have is one little cake, that is an awfully big request. Elijah makes a promise to her, though, that if she will share her cake, God will make sure that she never goes hungry or thirsty. He will provide for her.

Sharing is so hard to do, isn't it? But it is so important. Nobody in our world today needs to go hungry. All we would have to do to feed all the hungry people in the world is to get everybody else to share.

Of course, we not only share with other people, we also share with God. Every time the offering plate is passed we are sharing our money — our material abundance — with God. That's hard to do, too.

But God has made us a promise. If we will share with others, and if we will share with Him, He will provide us everything we need for happy, abundant lives. If we could believe that, really believe that, it would never be hard for us to share again.

BY FORCE OR BY FAITH?

Scripture Lesson: John 3:16
Object: A paper clip, some staples, and a stapler.

Boys and girls, can you tell me some ways that a paper clip and a staple are alike? I took this paper clip and these staples out of my desk. Say, that is one way they are similar. They are both used in an office. How else are they alike? They are both made out of metal, aren't they? What else? They serve a similar purpose, don't they? They are used to hold papers together. **(Take some papers and clip them together.)** See how easy that was. Now let's try the staples. First of all we need a stapler. **(Load the stapler.)** Now we put the corner of the papers under the stapler. Now, what do we do? That's right, we press down hard on the stapler until the staples go through the papers and hold them together. Boy, I would hate to get my hand under the stapler by mistake. That could hurt, couldn't it?

Now, let's forget about papers for a minute and think about God and us. It is God's greatest desire to join us together in love for one another and love for Him. He wants us all to be joined in love, peace, and harmony, together. That is God's will for His world. Now, if these papers represent our lives — if God wanted to join us together with one another and with Him — which do you think God would use — a paper clip or a staple? Would He try to force Himself upon us **(Strike the stapler hard.)** or would he gently wrap his arms about us. **(Put paper clip on papers.)** The Bible says, "God so loved the world . . . " If you love somebody, do you try to force yourself upon them? Of course you don't. Neither does God. He wants us to return His love. He wants us to be as one family, but He never forces us. He wants us to choose for ourselves.

JESUS LOVED PARTIES

Scripture Lesson: John 2:1-12
Object: A party hat.

I hope that you boys and girls don't make the same mistake that a lot of people make. A lot of people think that you have to have a long sad face in order to be a Christian. One little boy thought that. He was visiting an uncle who was a very religious man but who never smiled. He wasn't a very happy man to be around. That afternoon the little boy saw his uncle's mule out in the field. The mule, of course, had a long, sad face. "Poor mule," said the little boy. "You must be a Christian too."

Some people think you have to be solemn and somber to be a Christian. That is because they have not really understood what Jesus was like. Jesus was a man who loved to be with people. He was a man who enjoyed going to parties. He loved the beauty of His Father's creation. He used humorous language when talking to his disciples. He talked about an ugly old humped-back camel trying to squeeze through the eye of a needle. Can you even imagine that? He talked about people who were upset because some other person had a speck of dust in their eye while they themselves had a big piece of lumber in their eye.

Jesus said, "I have come that you may have life and have it more abundantly." That means it is His will for you to be happy and healthy. He wants us to enjoy our family and friends. He wants us to live in joyful harmony with God, with the world, and with other people.

THE PIG'S GREATEST MISTAKE

Scripture: Proverbs 22:1
Object: Picture of a pig (Miss Piggy from the Muppets would be good but do not let the children see the picture at first.)

I have a little quiz for you, boys and girls. It is a very little quiz. In fact there is only one question. Are you ready? What was *the* first native AMERICAN animal to be used in a circus? Think about that for a moment. Circuses are very old. There were circuses long before our nation was formed. And circuses have always used animals. Name some of them — lions, tigers, elephants, horses, dogs, etc. Now when circuses first started appearing in America, what was the first native American animal trained for a circus? **(Give them an opportunity to guess. Then unveil the picture of the pig.)**

Maybe you did not know that pigs are one of the smartest animals on earth. Of course sometimes they don't act too smart. If a pig has big, floppy ears, those ears may flop over into his eyes making him look clumsy. When we think of a pig we may think of wallowing in the mud — but the truth is that a pig prefers a clean surrounding. Somewhere, though, along the way the pig got a bad reputation — a reputation for being dumb and dirty. But they are not dumb or dirty.

Sometimes we can get a bad reputation. If we act selfish, or stuck-up, if we criticize others, or do mean things deliberately, we can get a bad reputation like those pigs. Pigs may be smart and fairly intelligent, but who wants to be thought of as a pig?

WHAT'S A BABY DOING IN A TREETOP?

Scripture Lesson: Psalm 116:6
Object: Some baby object (blanket, rattle, etc.)

I want you to think about a lullaby this morning. What is your favorite lullaby? Can you tell me what a lullaby is? That's right, it is a song — generally sung softly — for the purpose of helping a baby fall gently asleep. Now, can anyone think of a lullaby? **(Give the children ample opportunity to respond— even to sing a lullaby if they are so inclined.)**

The best known lullaby is probably one that goes like this:

> Rockaby (or hushaby) baby, in the treetop,
> When the wind blows the cradle will rock;
> When the bough breaks the cradle will fall,
> And down will come baby, cradle and all.

Have you ever wondered about the meaning of that little lullaby? What's a baby doing in a tree top in the first place? No one know for sure, because this little lullaby is over 100 years old. We think that perhaps the lullaby came from a custom of the Indians in the early days of our country. You know how how the Indian mothers carried their babies on their backs. Indian babies were snuggled in a kind of cradle made of birch bark. When the mothers were working they would hang the cradle with the baby inside on a nearby tree branch where the wind could rock it gently to sleep.

Indian mothers were careful to watch out over their little ones even while they worked. Our mothers and fathers don't carry us around on their backs or hang us on tree branches, but they watch over us while we are small. The Bible says that God is also "the keeper of the little ones." He too loves all the babies of this world.

HOW THE KANGAROO GOT ITS NAME

Scripture Lesson: Matthew 22:15-22
Object: The Bible.

Boys and girls,

Can somebody describe a kangaroo for us? That's right —
a large animal — has a pouch — what's the pouch for? That's
right, for carrying its young — it lives in Australia — has a big
tail. You know a lot about kangaroos, I can see. I was reading
something recently that I thought you might find interesting.
It was about how the kangaroo got its name.

An explorer named Captain Cook was in Australia many,
many years ago. He was talking with some of the natives of
Australia. They did not speak English, of course. They spoke
their own native language. Captain Cook was amazed when
he first got to Australia to see kangaroos hopping about, but
he didn't know what they were called. So he tried to explain
to the natives the animals he had seen and he asked them
what they were called. The natives weren't sure what Captain
Cook was asking so they answered, "Kangaroo," which in their
language meant, "What do you mean?" He thought they were
telling him the name of the animal, so ever since then they have
been called kangaroo. That's how the kangaroo got its name.
"What do you mean?" is what kangaroo really means.

Sometimes some of you who are in school have asked your
teacher, "What do you mean?" when you have not understood
something she has said. People were always asking Jesus, "What
do you mean?" Sometimes it was his own disciples asking him
about the meaning of one of his parables. Sometimes it was
the Pharisees trying to trick him.

Our object for today is simply our Bible. We study our Bible
to find out what Jesus meant. There is much about religion
we don't understand, so we read our Bibles and we come to
church and we pray, and slowly we grow to understand God's
plan for our lives. Kangaroo — "What do you mean?" That is
why we are here this morning — to try to understand.

GOD'S ABUNDANCE

Scripture Lesson: Romans 8:38-39
Object: A kernel of corn (an ear of corn would do better).

Boys and girls,

Our Scripture lesson is about God's love. I want to illustrate God's wonderful goodness through an ear of corn. You know that if you remove the covering to an ear of corn, you will find the corn's kernels. This is the part of the corn that we eat. It is also the part of the corn that we plant if we want more corn.

Now suppose I plant this one kernel. Soon it will grow and produce a stalk. On this corn stalk will grow two ears of corn. Each of the ears of corn will have 200 kernels on it. Now instead of one kernel, I have 400, from just one that I planted.

Suppose I plant all 400 of these new kernels. Now I have 400 stalks each with two ears, each of those with 200 kernels in them. Which means I now have —hold on to your hats — 160,000 kernels. And just one season ago I had one little kernel of corn.

If I plant each of those 160,000 kernels, I end up with 64 million kernels of corn. That is a lot of corn from one little kernel isn't it?

I am always amazed at how wonderful God's world is. Of course, this wonderful world shows us how wonderful God's love for us is. St. Paul tells us that nothing in the world can ever separate us from God's love. I believe that. If God can take one little kernel of corn and produce enough corn to feed everyone in the world, which is indeed possible, just think what he might be able to do with us if we loved Him as much as He loves us. There is no limit. So the next time you are eating corn, you might think about the amazing love of God found in one little kernel of corn.

GOD LOVES EVEN HUMMINGBIRDS

Scripture Lesson: John 3:14-21
Object: A feather, egg, or picture of a bird and a cross.

Boys and girls,

I am always amazed at God's love for the smallest of creatures. You remember that Jesus used a sparrow — a tiny bird — to show God's love. He said God's eye is on the sparrow, so, of course, God watches over us.

There is a bird smaller than a sparrow. It is the hummingbird. It is the tiniest of all birds. Have you ever seen a hummingbird? I imagine that Jesus would have used a hummingbird for his example, if he had ever seen one. You see, there were no hummingbirds in that part of the world. They only live in the western hemisphere. Hummingbirds are not only tiny, but they also make a humming sound, as you know. I'll bet you know the answer to the corny riddle, "Why do hummingbirds hum?" That's right. "They don't know the words."

Hummingbirds are not only tiny, but I understand that they also have very ugly tempers. If they get angry, they will attack any other bird or animal around. That's why I think Jesus might have talked about God's love for hummingbirds instead of sparrows if there had been any hummingbirds in that part of the world. Not only because they are smaller than sparrows but also because of their ugly tempers.

You see, sometimes we think God loves people only when they are good. The cross that Jesus died on tells us that God loves us even when we are bad. The cross is God's way of helping us move from having ugly tempers to loving others more. When we understand how much God loves us, then we are able to love others more.

So remember, God loves gentle little sparrows, but he also loves ugly-tempered hummingbirds. That is what the cross is all about. No matter who we are or what we do, we are still God's children.

THE POWER OF TOUCH

Scripture Lesson: John 20:19-31
Objects: A piece of sandpaper, and a piece of soft fur.

Boys and girls,

I want you to think about touch this morning. I have this piece of fur I want you to rub while I talk (**Have them pass it around.**) Notice how soft it is.

Now I want you to pass this piece of sandpaper. Notice how rough it is. Our sense of touch tells us many things. It tells us temperature. It warns us in case of a jagged object that might cut us. If we were blind, we might even depend upon our sense of touch to help us read or to guide us through a strange room.

In our scripture lesson for today, one of Jesus disciples named Thomas could not believe that Jesus had risen from the grave. "Unless I can touch him," said Thomas, "I cannot believe." For Thomas touching Jesus would prove that Jesus was really alive.

Of course there are many things in life that are real even though we can't touch them. Air is real. That's what we breathe. But we can't touch air. Love is real. You love your mother and father, but you can't touch love. You can touch someone you love. You can hug them and kiss them but you can't touch love. Love is something mysterious that comes from God.

Of course we can't touch God but God is real, just as real as you or me or the love we feel in our hearts. Thomas did get to touch the risen Christ but others knew Christ was risen who never touched him. They knew because his love was in their hearts.

A CHILD'S WITNESS

Scripture Lesson: Jeremiah 1:4-10
Object: A mirror.

(**Show the boys and girls the mirror, then look straight into it yourself.**) Let's see, boys and girls. I am holding in my hands the picture of a very handsome fellow, am I not? Oh, I'm not? Well you look into here and see if you do not see a very handsome fellow. (**pass the mirror around.**) Of course, some of you may see a very pretty girl. Why is that? Of course, this is a mirror. A mirror shows us the reflection of ourselves.

I want you to think for a few minutes this morning not about the mirror, but about the person you see in the mirror. That is, I want you to think about yourself. You know that God loves you. We've talked about that many times. God loves you more than you can imagine. Did you also know God wants you to be His partner? He wants to spread His love all over your school. He wants to spread His love all over your home. And He wants you to help Him do it.

Now in the Bible we read that God came to the prophet Jeremiah and told him to deliver a message for God to His people. Jeremiah tried to argue with God. "I am just a child he said . . . ." That is how you may feel. "I am just a child — how can I help God?" The Bible teaches us in many places that boys and girls are God's most important helpers. By your smiles, by your love, by your faith in Him, you can spread God's love everywhere. Why don't you try starting this morning?

DOES YOUR LABEL FIT?

Scripture Lesson: Matthew 7:16
Object: Jar of applesauce with a label from a pickle jar on it.

Boys and Girls:

Do we have any pickle lovers with us today? Oh, we do. That's great. As you can see I have a jar of pickles with me this morning. (show them the label that says "pickles." Take the lid off the jar and show the contents.) I am in a sharing mood this morning. I tell you what, let me share my pickles with you. (Offer the jar for anyone to take a "pickle.") What's the matter? I thought you liked pickles? (Let them respond.) What do you mean there's no pickles in this jar? It says "Pickles" right there. What do you think this is if it is not pickles? You think it is applesauce. Well, you're right. This morning before church I took the label off of a pickle jar and put it on this applesauce jar. That makes it kind of confusing, doesn't it? A jar that says "pickles" ought to have pickles in it.

Now there's a point to this. You and I don't wear signs that say that we are Christians. There's no label on our chest. Yet we are the people who bear the name of Jesus Christ. What if the people who are called Christian didn't act like Christians? Suppose they were mean and selfish and dishonest. Think how confusing that would be. A jar labeled pickles ought to have pickles in it. A Christian ought to show the love of Jesus in the way he or she lives.

TEMPTATION

Scripture Lesson: Romans 7:15
Objects: A banana and a box of vanilla wafers.

You know what this banana and these vanilla wafers remind me of — they remind me of banana pudding. They also remind me of the story of a great basketball player named Bill Russell. When Bill was a little boy his mother used to make great big bowls of banana pudding. How Bill loved that banana pudding. Does your mother ever make banana pudding? Hmm — I'll bet it's good. Well, Bill's mother made some banana pudding. And she left a big bowl of that pudding on the kitchen table. Then she and Bill's father went out for the afternoon. The last thing she said to Bill before she left was, "Don't you dare touch that banana pudding." Has your mother ever said something like that to you? "Don't you dare touch that banana pudding."

Well, Bill tried to resist that pudding. But it looked so good. Finally he thought to himself, "If I eat just a little bit around the edges no one will notice." So that is what he did. But after he did that he knew that his mother would know that he had been in the banana pudding, so he thought to himself, "You know, if I'm going to get punished anyway I might as well eat some more." Which he did. In fact, he ate the whole bowl full. Then he locked up the house and wouldn't let his parents in. He was afraid he would be punished.

Of course, he didn't need to be afraid of his parents. They would forgive him for eating the banana pudding. Why? That's right — because they loved him.

The Bible says that none of us do right all the time. But we have a loving Heavenly Father who forgives our sins.

AN EYEWITNESS ACCOUNT

Scripture Lesson: Luke 1:1-4; 4:14-21
Object: A Bible.

Let's suppose, boys and girls, that you and I were standing on the front steps of our church and a crime occurred. Suppose some men got into an argument and a fight was started and someone called the police. A few months later these men were put on trial because of the fight, and you and I were called to testify at the trial as eyewitnesses. Each of us would be marched up to the witness stand to give our testimony. We would put our hand on a Bible like this one and would promise to tell the truth and nothing but the truth. Did you know that even though we all saw the same things and even though we promised to tell the whole truth, the descriptions that we give about the fight would probably vary quite a bit. No two of us would likely remember the same thing. That is because each of us was noticing and hearing different things as the fight took place. Eyewitnesses rarely agree on all details.

That is true in our Bibles. We have four books in the Bible that tell about the life of Jesus. We call them the Gospels. Can you tell me what they are? That's right — Matthew, Mark, Luke, and John. All of them are based upon the testimony of eyewitnesses. But each of them tells the story a little differently. There is one thing all the eyewitnesses agree upon, however. Jesus of Nazareth was a very special man — the most special man who ever lived. He was so special that those who knew Him best, knew that he was the Son of God.

WHO BURST YOUR BUBBLE ?

Scripture Lesson: Luke 7: 1-10
Object: Enough bubble gum for each child to have a piece.

Boys and girls, if you will pardon me for a moment, I am going to chew a piece of bubble gum. **(Put a piece of bubble gum in your mouth and start chewing away.)** Now I would not want you to do this in a worship service, and I am going to have to find a graceful way to get rid of this piece immediately after our little talk. I will give you each a piece a little later for you to chew this afternoon if it is all right with your parents. A piece of bubble gum is a marvelous thing. You can just chew it like regular chewing gum or you can do what? That's right, you can blow a bubble **(now it is time for you to show your skill at blowing a bubble).** Of course you have to be careful when blowing a bubble, don't you? If you try to make the bubble too big, what will happen? That's right, it will burst and it might make quite a mess all over your face. I've had that to happen to me, have you? It can really be sticky, can't it? I've had another kind of bubble burst from time to time. That bubble is my pride. Sometimes we all get to thinking more of ourselves than we ought to. Our ego swells up like a big balloon or like a big bubble from a piece of bubble gum. And boy, it really hurts when somebody says something that pops my balloon or my bubble.

That's why it is dangerous when we start thinking that we are better than other people. Someone is always going to stick a pin in our bubble. Jesus really appreciated the centurion in our Scripture lesson. He was a humble man even though he was a powerful officer in the Roman army. He knew that every person is of equal value in God's eyes. That's the way for us to be. Not swelled up with hot air like this bubble **(blow another one).** But remembering that everyone we meet is also a child of God.

IT'S SOMETIMES FUN TO MOVE

Scripture Lesson: Luke 5:1-11
Object: A mover's box – a toy U-haul trailer – or some other object related to moving.

Have any of you ever had to move? Perhaps you have just moved from one house to another. Maybe you moved from one town to another. Maybe you've had to move from one part of the country to another.

Moving can be hard, can't it? There is all of the packing to do. But, even worse, there are all those friends to say good-bye to. Moving can be very lonely for us – particularly if we have been happy where we were.

Of course, moving can be fun, too. Moving into a new house – into a new neighborhood – making new friends – maybe even going to a new school. It's hard and yet if we make the best of it and ask God to help us have a cheerful attitude about it, moving can be quite exciting.

When the disciples of Jesus first met Him, they had to do some moving. The Bible tells us that they left everything and followed Jesus. It must have been hard for Peter to give up being a fisherman and for Matthew to give up being a tax-collector. But it must have been exciting too.

Sometimes it is hard for all of us to follow Jesus. He asks us to be more loving to other people. He asks us to always do the right thing even when others are doing wrong. Sometimes it's hard. But it is also exciting – knowing that He is our friend. Knowing that we don't have to be afraid – even in a new school, because we feel His love so near.

JESUS' GENTLE WAYS

Scripture Lesson: Luke 7:36 - 8:3
Object: A pitcher, a cup, and a large bowl.

Boys and girls, pardon me just a minute while I pour myself a drink of water. **(Pour from the pitcher to the cup fast enough so that some splatters out into the bowl.)** Oops, I guess I tried to pour the water too fast. Perhaps at home you have tried to fill a glass or a pan with water from a faucet and you turned the faucet on too hard. What happened then? The water probably splattered all over you and all over the kitchen as well. Sometimes we have to take our time and do things carefully and gently. Like filling this cup, if we try to force the water in too quickly, water just splatters all over the place.

That's one of the things I love about Jesus. He knew how to do things gently. For example, some of the people who wanted to follow Jesus were not very nice people. Like the lady in our Scripture lesson, other people in town looked down on them. The Pharisees wanted Jesus to tell people like that that they were no good. They wanted Jesus to try to force the sinners to be more righteous all at once. Jesus knew that wouldn't work. You don't help people improve by telling them that they are no good. You don't force people to try to change all at once. That's like trying to pour water into this cup too quickly. Jesus knew you have to work gently with people. You show them that you care about them and then you take one step at a time helping them to become what God wants them to become.

That's the way God deals with each of us. He doesn't make us become adults all at once. He gently leads us and helps us to grow. But He always loves us.

WHO SHALL TIE THE SHOE?

Scripture Lesson: Luke 3:7-18
Object: A shoe.

John the Baptist was a great man, boys and girls. He was one of the greatest preachers who ever lived. All of Jerusalem went out to hear him. If he were alive today, he would probably be more popular than all the famous preachers like Billy Graham and Oral Roberts combined. He was a great preacher. He was a great man of God. And yet John the Baptist said there was another preacher coming after him. *"Why, I'm not even worthy to tie his shoes!"* John the Baptist says. Do you know who John the Baptist was speaking about? That's right—he was talking about Jesus.

Suppose I were to ask for a volunteer this morning to come up out of our congregation to tie this shoe. But suppose I said this: In order to tie this shoe you must be as good as Jesus. Who do you think would be worthy to tie it? You know the answer, don't you? Nobody here — including you and including me is good enough. But that's alright. God knows that we are not Jesus. But he gave us Jesus so that by believing in Him and seeking to be like him as much as possible we might be God's people.

THE MORE YOU GIVE

Scripture Lesson: Luke 9:18 - 24
Object: A basket of candy.

Boys and girls, did you know that there are some things that the more you give, the more you have? Now that's not true about most things. For example, I have this basket of candy. I would like to give each of you a piece. **(Pass the basket and let each of them take a piece.)** Now, how much candy do I have left? I have less than I started with, don't I? But suppose my idea wasn't just to give you candy. Suppose what I really wanted to give you was happiness? I like to watch your eyes light up. I like to see you smile. It makes me happier to see you happy. So I have more happiness than I started with. The more happiness we give to others, the happier we are in return.

That's also true with friendship. If you want to have friends, then you have to be a friend. The more friendship we give to others, the more friendship we have. Of course, friendship is just another word for love. That's the nicest thing about love – the more we give, the more we have. That is the difference between spiritual blessings and material blessings.

Material blessings are like this candy. We can see the candy, we can feel it, we can taste it, but the more we give away to others, the less we have for ourselves. But spiritual blessings are just the opposite. Faith, hope, happiness, friendship, love – the more we give to others, the more we have for ourselves.

Jesus taught us that to save our lives, we must first lose them. That is what He was talking about. Your life is a spiritual quality. The more of that you give to God and to others, the more you will have for yourself. That is the key to the best life possible.

TIME TO SIT

Scripture Lesson: Luke 10:38-42   *used* 7/19/98
Object: A hoe and a book.

Boys and Girls:

A teacher once asked her pupils to draw a picture of their father working. Could you do that? What would you put in the picture? (**Give them a chance to answer.**) Well, some of the children in this class drew pictures of their father mowing the lawn, or hoeing in a garden, or driving a nail. But one little boy drew a picture of his father reading. The teacher asked him why he drew a picture of his father reading. The little boy answered that his father was a teacher in college and that part of his work was reading.

There are all kinds of work, aren't there? And work is very important. But there is a time to hoe in the garden and there's a time to read a good book. There's a time for work and for play and for rest and, as we learn in our Scripture lesson, a time for worship.

The Scripture lesson for today is about two women, Mary and Martha. Jesus was visiting in their home. Martha was a real worker. She kept hurrying and scurrying around the house waiting on her company. Her sister Mary, though, simply sat at the feet of Jesus. Martha complained to Jesus that Mary wasn't helping. Jesus, though, wanted Martha to know that there was something more important than work, or play, or rest — as important as they are. The most important hour in the week is the hour we spend in God's house — sitting at the feet of Jesus.

JOHNNY, WILLIAM AND ISAAC'S STORY

Scripture Lesson: Luke 13:1-9
Object: An apple.

We love apples, don't we, boys and girls? Red apples or golden yellow apples or even a green apple, if it is the right kind, are among the best fruits that God has given us. No wonder we all like the legend of Johnny Appleseed — the little man with a pan for a hat and a Bible by his side who went all over America doing — what? **(Let them answer.)** That's right, planting seeds.

The apple has always had a big place in legends. Do you remember the story about the man who had an apple fall on his head. What was his name? It was Sir Isaac Newton. We don't know if an apple really did fall on his head or not, but that is the tale people tell about how he discovered the law of gravity. Speaking of what people tell, can somebody tell me who William Tell was? That's right. He was the little boy who let his father shoot an apple off of his head. See how famous the apple is. What about in the Bible? Anybody remember a story that has an apple in it? The story of Adam and Eve? Well, the Bible doesn't really say it was an apple that Eve ate does it? But many of us like to think it was.

The apple is a kind of fruit, isn't it? It grows on trees. Fruit trees are very important in the Bible. In our Scripture lesson for the day, Jesus talked about fruit trees and he says that a fruit tree that does not bear fruit is not worth having. We can understand that, can't we? Why plant an apple tree if you don't plan on eating apples off of it. A fruit tree is only good if it bears fruit.

But Jesus wasn't talking just about fruit trees. He was talking about you and me. He wants us to bear fruit. He wants us to be what God created us to be — loving, kind, happy, sharing with one another. That's why He created us — to love one another and to love Him. So don't be like an apple tree with no apples. Make God happy by bearing his fruit of love and kindness.

ARE YOU LIKE A WATER HOSE?

Scripture Lesson: Luke 12:13-21
Object: A garden hose.

Boys and Girls:

Pardon me while I water my lawn. (**Wave the hose around as if using it.**) For some reason no water is coming out of this hose. I wonder why not? (**Let them tell you.**) Of course, that's my problem. My hose isn't connected to a faucet. But suppose it were connected. And suppose I put my thumb over the end and stopped up the hose. What would happen then? I still would not get any water, would I? Suppose there were something stuck in my hose so no water would pass through. My hose wouldn't be any good would it? What good is a hose if it won't let water through?

You know, we were created by God to be like a hose. His love is to pass through us to others like water through this hose. Jesus told about a man who was very selfish. He was very wealthy but he never thought about other people. He just wanted to eat, drink, and be merry. He wasn't a bad person. He was just a stopped up hose. And a stopped hose isn't worth much because the water can't flow through. Jesus called this man a fool because he did not pass God's love on to others.

Does God's love flow through you? If you were a hose would the water come spurting out or would it get clogged up by selfishness. How about passing God's love on today — to your parents, to your brothers and sisters, to your friends. Let His love flow freely through you.

WHEN YOU'RE HOOKED

Scripture Lesson: Matthew 4:1-11
Object: A fishhook and a cigarette.

Boys and girls, you know what temptation is, don't you? Let's suppose there are some of your favorite cookies on the kitchen table. Your mother is gone for the afternoon but you know she is saving the cookies for a party she is going to. You walk past the table and the cookies look so good. You think to yourself, "She won't miss just one cookie." And you are tempted to do something that you know you shouldn't do.

All of us are tempted at times. Jesus was tempted and he showed us that we can resist the temptor. But I would like to talk to you this morning about one particular temptation. (Bring out the cigarette.) What's this? It's a cigarette, isn't it? Some of you are getting to the age where you are going to be tempted to try smoking cigarettes. Most young people are tempted to try that sooner or later.

I hope you will be smart enough to realize that a cigarette is kind of like a fish hook. (Bring out the fishhook.) How many of you have ever been fishing? You know how a poor fish gets hooked and ends up in a frying pan, don't you? You cover the fish hook with some good looking bait. It doesn't look very good to you or me but it does to the fish. The fish is tempted by the bait and gets hooked.

Smoking cigarettes is like that. We think it makes us look cool to smoke, it makes us look grown up. And then like a poor fish we end up getting hooked and for the rest of our lives we ruin the insides of our body with cigarette smoke. Doctors tell us we will probably die way before we need to because we can't quit smoking.

God doesn't want you to be a fish. He wants you to be a human being. He wants you to be like Jesus. You can say "No!" to temptation because you realize that temptation usually has a hook underneath.

BUILDING HOUSES

Scripture Lesson: Luke 14:25-33
Objects: A child's sand pail and a set of blueprints.

Some of you may have gone to the beach this year. You probably enjoyed the waves and getting a good suntan and playing in the sand. Perhaps you built a sand castle. That's lots of fun, isn't it? You can take the moist sand and shape it into walls. Then perhaps you dug out a moat within the walls to protect your castle. Then you may have built a tower. It doesn't take much planning to build a sand castle, does it? It takes a little imagination and some patient construction, but not a whole lot of planning. But suppose you were building a real house. Wow! That is a different matter. You see these blueprints? Every little detail in building a house must be planned ahead of time — where the doors are going to go, what size windows will the house have, will it be brick or shingle, etc. It takes a specially trained person with a lot of skill and a lot of patience to draw up plans for a house.

But Jesus reminds us that some people are better at planning a house than they are planning a life. Some people, who would be very careful if they were building a house to plan every detail, never stop to think about the rest of their life and where they are headed. Now which is more important, building a house or building a life? Of course, building a life. So let's give some thought to our lives. Let's make sure that our lives are built on a strong foundation — especially the foundation of Jesus' love for us and our love for one another.

LESSON FROM A COIN

Scripture Lesson: Luke 15:1-32
Object: A coin

Boys and girls, what am I holding in my hand? It is a coin, isn't it? It is a piece of money. Do you think Jesus ever talked about money. Yes, he did. In fact he talked about money just about more than he did any other subject. That is because money is a very important subject in our lives. We need money to buy food and clothes and gas for our cars and what else? **(Give them a chance to name some things they buy.)**

Can you think of two occasions when Jesus used a coin like this one to teach a lesson? Remember when someone asked Jesus about paying taxes to the government? He took a coin like this one and asked them a question: "Whose picture is on this coin?" he asked. They answered, "Caesar's." Jesus told them — what? That's right. "Render unto Caesar the things that are Caesar's and unto God the things that are God's."

But there is another important time when he used a coin to teach a lesson. It is found in today's scripture lesson. A certain woman had a very valuable coin. And it fell behind some furniture in her house and she could not find it. So what did she do? She swept the whole house to find that one lost coin, and when she found it she was so excited she just couldn't wait to tell her friends about it.

Jesus said that you and I mean a lot more to God than that coin meant to that woman. We can make God very happy just by giving ourselves to Him. Remember that the next time you have a coin in your pocket. Think not only about the ice cream or candy bar you are going to buy. Remember also how much God loves you.

THREE REMINDERS OF GOD'S LOVE

Scripture Lesson: Luke 15:1-32
Objects: A coin, a toy lamb (or a picture of a lamb) and a mirror.

Boys and girls, in the fifteenth chapter of St. Luke, Jesus tells us three stories in order to help us understand God's love for us. The first story is about a coin — a coin that was so precious (**show the coin to the children**) that a woman swept out her whole house when she discovered that it was lost. She swept her whole house in order to find that coin and when she found it — she was so happy that she rushed next door to tell her friends.

Jesus also told about a little lost lamb. (**Hold up lamb.**) The shepherd had 99 other sheep but he missed this one lost lamb and when he found it, he was very happy.

But there is a third story. This mirror might remind us of that story. (**Pass the mirror and let them look into it.**) What do you see in this mirror? You see yourself, don't you? The third story Jesus told was about a lost boy. It could have been a lost girl, though. The story would have been the same. The boy wandered off from home. But one day he came back — and, oh, his father was so happy. He was so happy that he threw a party.

Jesus said that God is like that woman looking for her coin. He is like that shepherd searching for his little lamb. He is like the father gazing down the road for his lost boy to come home. God's one wish in this world is for us to give him our hearts so that He may give us great joy in return. And so He is waiting and calling and looking for us.

CRUMBS FROM THE TABLE

Scripture Lesson: Luke 16: 19-31
Objects: A piece of bread and a washcloth.

When do you wash your hands, boys and girls? Before a meal or afterwards? Usually we wash our hands before a meal. But suppose we did not have a knife or a fork or a spoon? Suppose we had to eat with our fingers? I imagine at one time or another that all of us did eat with our fingers. Some of you may have a younger brother or sister who is messier after a meal than before. Your mother may have to take a washcloth and wash off the baby's hands and face after the meal as well as before.

Jesus told about a poor man named Lazarus who sat at the gate of a very rich man named Dives. The rich man had every good thing in the world to eat. But poor Lazarus had nothing. Jesus said that Lazarus was waiting for the crumbs of bread that fell from Dives table. At this particular time in history, William Barclay, the English Bible scholar says, there were no knives or forks or napkins. In the homes of the very wealthy, the hands were cleaned by wiping them on hunks of bread — and then the bread was thrown away. It was this bread that Lazarus waited to eat.*

That seems like a very unsatisfactory way to wash your hands, doesn't it? A wash cloth is a much better way. But the story of the rich man and Lazarus is not a story about how we wash our hands. It is a story about caring for other people. Lazarus was very poor. He sat at the rich man's gate begging for food. But the rich man never noticed him. Jesus tells us that we are to notice people and care about people — particularly those who are not as fortunate as we are.

From a sermon by Carl R. Bowser, Ballard United Methodist Church, Asbury Park, New Jersey.

THE PROBLEM WITH GREED

Scripture Lesson: Luke 16:1-13
Object: A jar with a mouth just large enough for a child's hand.

This object lesson is based on a sermon by Dwight L. Moody and can be very effective in dramatizing greed. The mouth of the jar needs to be just large enough to admit a child's hand. Have a coin in the bottom of the jar. Have a volunteer put a hand into the jar, clutch the coin and make a fist. Then have the person remove their hand. If the jar is the right "fit" the child's hand will not come out while clenched in a fist. **(You may have to try several volunteers before you find the one whose hand becomes stuck.)** Make the point then that in order to remove the hand, the fist has to be unclenched, losing the coin but regaining the hand. Then tell the children Jesus' teaching on serving God and mammon .

THE POISONOUS "LOVE APPLE" [1]

Scripture Lesson: John 8:1-11
Object: A tomato (hidden at first).

I want to offer you an exotic piece of fruit, boys and girls, cultivated first high in the Andes mountains of South America. It was some Indian who discovered this luscious red fruit growing on a vine. He was afraid to eat it at first. But he did. It had a most unusual taste. But it was good. So he picked some of this fruit and took it home. Others liked it so well that they started saving the seeds and planting them. Soon the little red fruit was growing all over South America. Then the Spaniards conquered South America and they started taking the seeds of this little red fruit home to Spain. Soon the little red fruit was growing all over Europe.

Finally in the first half of the 19th century — a little over 150 years ago — the seeds of this little red fruit made its way to the United States. But do you know what? There were a lot of people in this country who were afraid to eat this little red fruit. They were afraid it was poisonous. In fact they called it the poisonous "love apple." Now it wasn't an apple at all though it is about the same size. And it most certainly is not poisonous though I understand some people may be allergic to it. What it might have to do with love, I don't know. But that's what they called it — the poisonous love apple. Many people were afraid to eat it. You know what kind of fruit this poisonous love apple was? (**Let them guess — then bring out the tomato.**) That's right, it was a tomato.

Those of us who like tomatoes on our hamburgers and in our salads can't imagine people thinking it was poisonous. Sometimes people are that way. Sometimes we all look for the worst. We are so different from Jesus. He always looked for the best in people — even this woman in our Scripture lesson who had done something very wrong. He saw the best in her. He forgave her sin and told her to be a better person from now on. He sees the best in each one of us, too. And He wants us to be our best.

---

[1] Cf. *Behold The Glory,* Chad Walsh (New York: Harper & Brothers, 1955).

WHY IS IT CALLED A WOODCHUCK?

Scripture Lesson: Mark 12: 28-34
Object: A name tag that says "Christian."

Boys and girls,

We used to say a little tongue-twister that I'll bet you know too: "How much wood would a woodchuck chuck if a woodchuck would chuck wood?" I started wondering: Why are woodchucks called woodchucks?

In the dictionary we discover that a woodchuck is the same thing as a groundhog. They are simply called different names in different parts of the country. The encyclopedia tells us that a woodchuck is about 2 feet long, including its bushy tail, and that it builds very complex burrows in the ground where it spends most of its time when it is not out looking for food. That explains why it is called a groundhog. Woodchucks eat plants like alfalfa and clover and sometimes can be destructive to gardens. Woodchucks also hibernate in the winter.

None of that explains why they are called woodchucks, which leaves me very confused about the tongue-twister, "How much wood would a woodchuck chuck if a woodchuck would chuck wood?"

I believe somebody somewhere sometime just gave woodchucks a wrong name.

Now then, you and I are called "Christians." Is that a good name for us? I hope it is. A Christian is simply a follower of Jesus--somebody who seeks to love God with all his heart, soul, mind and strength, and tries to love other people as much as he loves himself. Does that description fit you? I hope it does. I hope none of us is like the woodchuck and has a name that just doesn't fit.

FROM A TINY SEED

Scripture Lesson: Luke 17:1-10
Objects: A package of seed and a piece of bark from a large tree (also an acorn if one is available).

Boys and girls:

There is an old story about a tiny acorn that had great dreams. He was tiny now, but one day he would be a giant oak tree spreading his limbs and casting an impressive shadow over everyone around him. Someday perhaps someone would come and cut him down and shape him into a giant sailing ship or perhaps a beautiful home. This tiny little acorn had all these great dreams. A little sparrow who was a friend of his asked him if he really believed he would accomplish all that. "Yes," replied the little acorn, "God and I will."

This little story reminds us of two important lessons. First of all, everything that is great in this world started out as a little seed. This piece of bark I took from a great tree. But years ago it was a tiny seed about the same size as these seeds. Every great thing starts out as a tiny seed. Sometimes that seed is just a dream in somebody's heart. And they believe in that dream. And they keep working until that dream comes true.

The second thing this little story reminds us is that growth always comes from God. The little sparrow asks the tiny acorn if he will really accomplish all that, and the little acorn replies, "Yes, God and I will!" There is a great lesson for life. A person and God can accomplish great things. Whether it is at school or with your friends, or simply trying to be the kind of people we want to be, God's help can make all the difference in the world.

THE MOST IMPORTANT LAWS

Scripture Lesson: John 13:31-35 2 Lead C fail to story
Object: An important looking document or scroll. is unrelated to this text

Boys and girls, let's use our imaginations this morning. Let's pretend that a group of scientists have been looking through some caves around the Dead Sea. Does anybody know where the Dead Sea is? It's in Israel near where Jesus lived and taught 2,000 years ago. Do any of you know why it is called the Dead Sea? That's right. It has no outlet. Water comes into it, but cannot get out. The water sits there until it evaporates in the hot sun. The minerals and acids in the water have settled to the bottom and killed off all the fish and plant life. That is why it is called the Dead Sea.

Several years ago some scientists did find some very important scrolls in one of the caves around the Dead Sea. These scrolls date all the way back to Jesus' time, and have been very helpful in understanding the world in which Jesus lived.

But suppose a new team of scientists went out today, and suppose they found one document and on that document they found written the two most important laws ever written. What do you suppose those two laws would be? Well, Jesus has already told us what those two laws would be, hasn't he? The first one is that we should love God. And the second is what? That's right. We should love one another.

Sometimes we forget how important it is that we love one another. Yet that is how people can know that the love of Jesus is in our hearts. Remember that this week at school. Others will know how much you love God by how you treat the people around you.

STAR WARS REVISITED

Scripture Lesson: Colossians 1:1 - 20
Object: A picture, toy, shirt, helmet, etc. with the Star Wars insignia on it.

Boys and girls:

The Empire Strikes Back. That's big news for the summer, isn't it, boys and girls? Darth Vader is back. It's *Star Wars* all over again. That's big news.

Well, I've got bigger news for you. There is someone who is in control over all of the empires of outer space. Here is how one book describes Him:

> **For by him were all things created, that are in heaven, and that are in earth, visible and invisible, whether they be thrones, or dominions, or principalities, or powers: all things were created by him and for him.** (Colossians 1:16)

Wow! That is big news, isn't it? That means He's bigger and stronger than anything or anybody in this galaxy or any other galaxy. He's not only bigger and stronger, but He even created everything in this universe and everything in outer space.

But, you know, even though He is bigger and stronger, He never uses His power in a mean or evil way. In fact, He always tries to help. He is concerned about a tiny sparrow that doesn't even show up on a radar screen flying through the earth's atmosphere. And he cares about you and me. Who am I talking about? **(Let them answer.)** Of course, it's God. He is the God of all outer space as well as of this universe. And yet we can pray to Him and call him, **Our Father.**

A CAR WITHOUT GAS

Scripture Lesson: Colossians 1:11
Object: A gasoline can.

Boys and girls:

We all know what this is, don't we? It is a gasoline can. We put that very expensive stuff that runs our cars in this can.

Suppose someone gave you the most beautiful car ever built. Suppose it was your favorite color. Suppose it was air-conditioned and had a CB radio and power windows and a tape deck. Suppose everything on it worked — the windshield wipers, the clock, the battery and so on. Suppose it had very expensive radial tires and a powerful motor under the hood. What else could it have that I may have forgotten? **(Let them suggest some things for the car.)** Now, suppose you had this beautiful car. It was all yours. You're ready to take it out on a long trip. But suddenly you discover that you don't have any gas. This beautiful car. It's all yours. But you can't go anywhere because you have no gasoline to power the engine.

Did you know that there are some people who are like that automobile. They are nice-looking people. They have nice faces and strong bodies. They have good minds and do well in school or at work. On the outside they look like they have it made. On the inside, though, they feel very empty and alone. They don't know why they are even alive. They are good-looking automobiles with no gasoline. They have no power in their lives — the power that comes from knowing that God is alive in their hearts. You and I can have that power though. God has promised it to us. All we have to do is open our hearts and let Him come into us and fill us with His love and goodness.

CALL THE WATCHMAKER

Scripture Lesson: Hebrews 4:12-16
Object: A watch or clock.

There is a famous clock in a large cathedral in Strasburg, Germany. When it was built it was so complicated that the only one who knew how to fix it was the man who had built it. He was angry at the people of Strasburg because they were slow in paying him. So one day he slipped up to the tower and touched some secret springs and the great clock stopped. No one could figure out how to start the clock again. Finally the people of the town paid the builder of the clock and he went back to the tower and started the clock running again.

You know, boys and girls, you and I are like that great clock. No one really understands why we do some of the things we do. I wish that I could say that I knew all the answers, but I don't. Why do some of us enjoy hurting other people? Why do we do foolish things that might even cause us to hurt ourselves? No doctor can answer that question, no lawyer, no psychologist. There is only One who understands why we do the things we do. That is the One who made us. That One, of course, is who? That's right, God.

That is why we need to go to Him daily in prayer. He can help fix us on the inside. When we are sad, He can make us glad. When we are angry, he can calm us again. We are the clock. He is the clockmaker. We need His care if we are to run smoothly.

NO BEGINNING AND NO END

Scripture Lesson: Revelation 1:4-19
Object: A wedding band (Hands clasped covering wedding band.)

Boys and girls, I have something on the third finger of my left hand that is very important to me. Would you like to guess what it is? That's right. It is a wedding band. What does that mean? It means that I am married. It means that once upon a time my wife and I stood before God and some persons and made a vow to love and honor one another "until death us do part." That band is very important to me. It symbolizes one of the most important vows that I have ever taken.

Now it is important that the wedding band is circular. A circle is a symbol for eternity. If we say that something is eternal, what do we mean? It means that it has no end. St. Paul tells us that love is eternal. It has no end. Where is the end of this wedding band of gold? It has no end, does it? It just goes round and round. That is why a circle is a good symbol for eternity.

God gives us two more symbols in the book of *Revelation*. He says, "I am the Alpha and the Omega . . ." Do you know where the words Alpha and Omega come from? They are the first and the last letters in the Greek alphabet. In fact that's where we get the word alphabet — from the first Greek letter "alpha." What are the first and last letters in our alphabet? That's right, "A" and "Z". So God says to us, "I am the A and the Z. I am the beginning and the end." God has no beginning and no ending. He is forever. We can't even imagine what forever is like — but aren't you glad that someone who loves us as much as God does will always and forever be with us? I am.

WORTHY OF OUR PRAISE

Scripture Lesson: Revelation 5:6-14
Object: A hymnal, prayer book, or other book of worship.

The word picture in the book of *Revelation* is beautiful, boys and girls. In a vision the writer of the book, a man named John on the island of Patmos, sees the Lamb of God.

Who is the Lamb of God? That's right. The Lamb of God is a symbol for Jesus. John sees the Lamb of God and hears thousands of voices — every creature on earth and in heaven sing "Worthy is the Lamb . . . To Him who sits upon the throne and to the Lamb be blessing and honor and glory and might forever and ever!" Isn't that a beautiful scene? Everything in heaven and on earth praising God and praising Christ singing, "Worthy is the Lamb."

That is where we get our word "worship." When we worship God we are saying "Worthy is the Lamb." When we sing our hymns in our worship service and have our prayers and read the Scriptures, it is our way of saying to Christ, "We praise you. We love you. We thank you for all the blessings you have given us. You are the most important thing in our lives. Without you we are nothing."

That is why worship is so important. That is why we should never come into worship with a glum face. Just like in the book of *Revelation*. Just like in John's Vision. On this day all of God's people gather together to praise Him. It should be a joyful occasion. It should be a time of celebration. "Worthy is the Lamb . . . " He is worthy isn't He? He is so loving and so good. He cares about us so much. Worthy is the Lamb to receive our worship.

WIPING AWAY TEARS

Scripture Lesson: Revelation 7:9-17
Object: A sand bucket and shovel.

Boys and girls, let me tell you a story about a little boy named Tommy who went one summer day to the beach with his mother and father. It was a beautiful sunny day, and Tommy had been looking forward to going to the beach for such a long time.

He loved to play in the sand. He had his bucket and shovel with him, and today he was determined to build the biggest and most beautiful sand castle ever built.

When they finally arrived at the beach, Tommy immediately jumped out of the car and ran to look for a place to build his castle. The beach was crowded, but finally he found a good spot and went right to work. With great loving care he began to construct the walls and the towers. How proudly his castle would stand! He knew that it would be the finest on the beach that day.

Unfortunately, Tommy was working so studiously on his castle that he did not notice that the water from the ocean was coming toward his castle. What was happening? That's right — the tide was coming in. All of a sudden Tommy's feet started getting wet. Then a small wave toppled one of the walls of his castle. Then he stood there helplessly while one of his proud towers was swept away.

A tear trickled down Tommy's face. Tommy's father saw what was happening, and he said, "Don't cry, Tommy, it's just a sand castle. It's not really important." But Tommy's mother was wiser. She knew that it was important. She came over and put her arms around Tommy and wiped the tear from his eye. And Tommy was glad that she understood.

Boys and girls, the Bible tells us God is like Tommy's mother. He understands the things that are important to us. He understands the things that hurt us. And one day he will wipe every tear from our eyes.

FISH STORIES

Scripture Lesson: Jonah 3:1-5, 10
Object: A bowl of goldfish or a picture of a fish.

Fish are very important to our lives. For millions of the world's people, fish is their most important food. Fish also make good pets. They don't make much noise. They don't eat much. They're nice to watch.

Fish are important in the Scriptures. You remember the large fish that swallowed a certain prophet. What was that prophet's name? That's right. His name was Jonah. You will also remember the young boy who had two loaves of bread and five tiny fish. What did Jesus do with those loaves and fishes? That's right. He fed 5,000 people, didn't he?

Jesus knew about fish. He gave some of his friends advice on fishing. They were very tired and discouraged. They had been fishing all night and had not caught anything. Jesus told them to cast their nets on the other side of the boat. They did and they brought in an abundance of fish.

Yes, Jesus knew about fishing. He also knew the story about the Prophet Jonah staying in the belly of the large fish three days. When he was about your age, he probably learned that story in the synagogue. Later as he faced his death, he recalled that story and he said that he would be in the tomb for three days just as Jonah was in the fish for three days before God would raise him from the dead.

Jesus remembered as an adult the stories he learned as a little boy. You will too, someday. It might be when you are very afraid and you might remember the story of Daniel and the lion's den. Then you will think, God will help me like he did Daniel or like he did David when he faced Goliath. Bible stories are important. Even stories about fish are important. They tell us that God is always with us. We are not alone. God loves us and He is with us.

FISHERS OF MEN

Scripture Lesson: Mark 1:14-20
Object: A fishing rod.

Last week we talked about the importance of fish. But suppose we wanted to catch a fish. What would we need? That's right — a fishing rod.

Some of Jesus' friends were fishermen. That was how they earned their living. They owned boats and large nets. They depended on the sea for their living. Jesus offered them a new job, though. "Come with me," he said, "and I will make you fishers." What do you think he meant by that? O.K. That's right. Instead of catching fish, they were going to catch men. Not with a rod and reel, I hope. I would hate to have a fish hook in my mouth, wouldn't you? No, he didn't mean that they were going to catch men in the same way you catch fish. Not with a rod and reel. Yet they did become great fishers of men. Those twelve early disciples **(with one replacing Judas after he betrayed Jesus)** would one day reach thousands of men, women, and children and help them become Christians. Just as they hauled in their nets with thousands of fish when they were fishermen, they brought in thousands of persons into the Christian faith.

How did they do it? Not with a rod and reel, of course. They did it with preaching and teaching and praying. But most of all they did it with love. They knew how to love one another. If someone was in trouble they would help them. If someone needed a friend, they would be a friend.

That's what God wants each of us to do, boys and girls. That's the most important job in the church — to love one another. To find someone who needs a friend and to be a friend. To help people who need help. Then we can be fishers of men too.

BEGIN WITH BAPTISM

Scripture Lesson: Mark 1:4-11 (The Baptism of Jesus)
Object: A picture of a lake or ocean

A boy from the Middle West who had never before seen the ocean made a trip to the West Coast. As he looked out across the vast Pacific, he stood quietly. "Well," asked a friend, what do you think of it?" "It's wonderful," replied the boy, "but I hate to see all that water out there doing nothing."

That is how an ocean might look to us − like it is doing nothing. But there is tremendous power in an ocean. In fact, one of the newest ways in which they are experimenting to find more energy is to try to harness the ocean's tides. I don't know how they plan on doing that, but an ocean does not just sit there. Even when it looks calm, something great is going on.

If someone had seen the river Jordan the day Jesus was baptized, they might have said, "How lazy the river looks. I hate to see all that water sit there doing nothing." Little could they know that something was going to happen in the river Jordan that would change the history of the world.

Jesus of Nazareth was baptized in the river Jordan. And the Holy Spirit came upon him in the form of a dove. Jesus had been a carpenter, but now he would leave the carpenter shop to teach and to heal and to fulfill the purpose God had for him. But first he had to be baptized. It was his baptism that marked a new beginning.

That is why when a person gives his life to Jesus, the first thing we ask him or her to do is to be baptized. This is our initiation. This says 'I belong to the family of Christ.' Baptism says that 'I am going to make a new beginning too − walking in the footsteps of Christ.'

THE WORD BECAME FLESH

Scripture Lesson: John 1:1-18
Object: Several translations of the Bible.

I have several different versions of the same book this morning. I imagine that you have already guessed what book that is. That's right — the *Bible*. I have here a King James version — that's the version with all the "thees and thous." It is written in old English. It is a very beautiful version and for many people it is the only Bible they will accept.

These other Bibles are more modern translations. This Bible — the *Living Bible* — reads just like a story book. There is one translation of the *Bible* that is written especially for children.

Unfortunately most people never read a Bible. Most of your friends probably do not read a Bible. How will they know what the Christian faith is all about? How will they know how much God loves them? I know. They could see it in you and me. If we live the way Jesus wants us to live, then the world will know about God's love. They will see that love in our warm smiles.

God knew that most people would never read His Word. So he sent Jesus to be the Word. The *Bible* says, **"The Word became flesh and dwelt among us."** Now Jesus wants us not only to read His word but to be His word. If our friends never read a Bible, they can still know God's word, because it lives in us.

FLOWERS

Scripture Lesson: II Corinthians 12:7-10

A recent magazine article told about flowers in church. Did you know that in some churches flowers are chosen according to the theme for the day? The flowers, besides adding beauty to the sanctuary, become important symbols. For example, if the theme for the day is "love," the flowers might be roses. If the theme is to be the unity of the church, a grapevine might somehow be used to remember how Jesus once compared himself to a grapevine and us to the branches. An arrangement of oak leaves might signify God's faithfulness, and one of the palms could stand for victory.

Flowers are a constant reminder to us of God's love for us. When Jesus wanted to get his disciples to trust God more, he said to them: "Consider the lilies of the field; they neither toil nor spin; yet I tell you that Solomon in all his glory was not arrayed as one of these." (Matthew 6:28-29)

Of course, being human beings, we sometimes forget to trust in God. Love is sometimes very hard. Things happen at school and at home that make us very sad. But soon the sun shines again. Because God does not forget his promise to always be with us.

THE WIDOW'S MITE

Scripture Lesson: II Corinthians 8:1-15

Once there was an elderly woman who was very poor. Her husband was dead and she had barely enough income from the small amount of work that she was able to do to buy food to eat and clothes to wear. But once a week she went to the temple to take her offering to God. Others lived in nicer houses than she did, but that didn't bother her either. She was a little embarrassed when the collection was taken, however. Many wealthy people brought large gifts of money and all she could put in were two small coins of very little value. She dropped her eyes in embarrassment as her time came.

She did not know that someone was watching her as she dropped her coins into the plate. It was Jesus. He watched with love and appreciation and said to his disciples: "This poor widow has cast more in than all who have cast into the treasury."

Your gift is important to God. It may be very small, but if it means that you love God and are willing to sacrifice in order to share in his work, God will bless your gift and you.

CONTAGIOUS HAPPINESS

Scripture Lesson: Mark 6:7-13
Object: A thermometer.

How many of you have had the measles? How about mumps or chicken pox? It's not much fun to have one of these diseases, is it? Probably you caught one of these diseases from somebody else. And maybe you gave one of these diseases to someone else. That's because these are contagious diseases. Contagious means they can be passed from one person to another. It's not too nice to pass something painful like mumps, is it?

There are some good things that are contagious. Happiness is one of these. Happiness can be passed from one person to another. If you don't believe that, try it tomorrow. Or try it when you go home after church today. See how much happiness you can spread today.

Jesus sent his disciples out two by two to spread his love in the world. Today he means for you and me to spread his love. Let's be contagious Christians, why don't we? Instead of spreading measles and mumps and chicken pox, though, let's spread love and joy and peace.

2 PLUS 2

Scripture Lesson: Deuteronomy 4:32 - 34; 39 - 40
Object: A pocket calculator.

What if I were to say to you that 2 plus 2 makes 3? Would I be right? How about if I said 2 plus 2 equal 5? What does 2 plus 2 equal? That's right, 4. That will never change, will it? How about if we took a vote on it? That wouldn't change it either. Two plus two will always equal four. There are some things that it does no good to vote on.

Right and wrong are like that. Have you ever said to your mother: "Everybody else in my class gets to do such and such." Just because everybody else does something doesn't mean it is right does it? Some things are just right and other things are just wrong - regardless of what anybody says about them.

The Bible helps us to know the difference between right and wrong. It teaches that anything that hurts other people, hurts ourselves, or hurts our relationship with God is wrong. That is important to know because when we do right, we enjoy life more and we help others to enjoy life more.

FOOTBALL

Scripture Lesson: Ephesians 4:1
Object: A football.

With football season only a short time away, perhaps it is a good time for us to be reminded that being a Christian is like being an athlete. The athlete works out daily. He keeps his body in excellent condition. If he is truly dedicated, he will make many sacrifices and devote much hard work to be at his best in every game.

Our Christian faith calls for us to take care not only for our bodies but our minds and hearts as well. It calls for us to make sacrifices and to devote much hard work in serving God. Our faith includes a daily workout as well. There should be a time each day when you turn your thoughts entirely toward God. It may be as you kneel beside your bed each night. Or it may be as you read the Bible.

Think about this in the coming week. Like a football player you are in training. You are part of God's team in the game of life. And He wants you to be your best!

LONDON BRIDGE

Scripture Lesson: Ephesians 2:11-22
Object: A family Bible.

Boys and Girls:

Have you ever sung the song, *"London Bridge is Falling Down?"* You may have read not too long ago that they tore down the London Bridge and moved it to Arizona. It cost $7 million dollars to dismantle it and to ship the 10,246 numbered pieces across the ocean where they put it together again in Lake Havashu City, Arizona for a tourist attraction. It seems kind of silly, doesn't it, to spend all that money on a bridge just to look at?

Some families have in their homes a Bible that is no more than a "tourist attraction." They leave it on a table where it can be seen but they never actually use it. They never read it or study it or let it guide their living. That's kind of silly, too, isn't it?

A Bible is to be used. God speaks to us when we study His word. In fact, the Bible can be a bridge on which we travel in order to get to God, because the Bible teaches about Jesus, and Jesus is the cornerstone upon which our lives in God are built.

YOUR WONDERFUL HEART

Object: Paper Valentine.

What is this, boys and girls? It is a valentine, or a paper heart. It signifies love, doesn't it? But I would like for you to think about another heart.

If I told you to be perfectly still for a moment, you would find it impossible. Parts of you are still moving even while you are standing quietly with your hands at your side. For example, your heart is still beating. Have you ever thought about your heart? It is a marvelous machine. Did you know that in a normal life-span your heart will beat 800,000,000 times? Somebody figured out that in that 800,000,000 beats, your heart will pump enough blood to fill a string of railroad tank cars from New York to Boston. That is almost unbelievable, is it not?

The Bible talks a lot about the heart. But it is not talking about the heart that pumps all the blood. When the Bible talks about the heart, it is generally referring to our thoughts and feelings.

The Bible tells us that God wants a dwelling place in our hearts. That is, our thoughts and feelings are to be in tune with God's thoughts and feelings. Then we discover what Jesus meant when he said, "Blessed are the pure in heart, for they shall see God."

CREATION

Object: A picture of a bird.

Does anyone know what kind of bird this is? (**Let them guess.**) Does anybody remember when Jesus talked once about a certain kind of bird? What kind of bird was it? It was a sparrow.

It is interesting that Jesus chose a bird when he wanted to express the Father's concern for our physical need. Professor J. A. Carlson in an article entitled *"Your Body,"* speaks of hunger. He notes that a bird can go nine days without food. A man twelve days. A dog twenty days. A turtle, five hundred days. A snake eight hundred days. A fish one thousand days. Insects twelve hundred days.

Birds and humans — they are among the most fragile of God's creatures. That's why Jesus chose the sparrow to teach his lesson about God's love. Jesus said God knows when a tiny sparrow falls from the sky. If He cares about a tiny bird, wouldn't he even more care about you and me?

THE TWO-TOED SLOTH

Scripture Lesson: I Peter 3:18-22
Object: A book—your Bible will do—held upside down.

Boys and girls,

I want to read to you from this book, but something is wrong. **(Show them the upside down book.)** Can somebody tell me what's wrong with this book? That's right— it's upside down. What if you lived in a world that was upside down?

I read about an animal that spends most of its life upside down. It's called a two-toed sloth. I've never seen one, but I understand that they are quite large. They live in trees and, for the most part, live their lives upside down. They eat, sleep and even travel through the forest upside down. What a strange world they must live in — living upside down.

That's what the Bible tries to keep us from doing. Oh, I don't mean that the Bible tries to keep us from walking on our hands. What I mean is that the Bible shows us the things that are good — like loving God and our fellowman — like taking care of our bodies, minds, and souls — like living in harmony with this beautiful world — and the Bible says to us, "Live according to these rules — right side up — and you will find happiness and peace."

But some people try to live upside down. They ignore God. They mistreat other people. They mess up their bodies, minds and souls, they treat the world like a big trashpile, and they wonder why they are so miserable. They are miserable because they are living upside down. They are not living the way God wants them to live — right side up. If you live like the way God wants you to live, it's like walking on your feet rather than on your hands.

THIS IS MY SON

Transfiguration
2/14/99

Scripture Lesson: Matthew 17:1-9
Object: A price tag.

Boys and girls, have you ever been to an auction? Somebody tell us what an auction is? **(Let one of the children explain.)** I heard about an auction where just for a joke the auctioneer took a small boy from the audience and placed him up on the stage and asked the crowd, "How much am I bid for this young man? Five dollars? Ten dollars? Fifteen dollars. Who'll start the bidding?" Then a man spoke up from the crowd. "There's not enough money in all the world to buy that boy," he said. "Why not?" asked the auctioneer." "Because," said the man, "that's my son."

I brought a price tag with me this morning. I could put it on one of you and we could have an auction. But I can guarantee you that there is not enough money in all the world to buy you from your parents. You are the most important person in all the world to them.

Our reading from the Bible tells about a time when Jesus was on the mountain with three of his disciples when they heard a voice from heaven say, "This is my beloved son." Jesus was God's son. He was worth more than all the money in the world to God. There was only one thing in the world for which God would give up Jesus. The Bible tells us that God gave Jesus up for us. Jesus was crucified on a cross because of God's love for us. We don't understand why that was necessary, but we do know that God must love us a great deal to give up his son for us.

ON LOAN

Scripture Lesson: Luke 6: 17-26
I Cor. 15: 12-20

Object: A library book.

Boys and girls,

I have a very special book with me this morning. Does anybody know what makes this book special? *(Let them suggest some possibilities. Then show them the numbers on the binding.)* Now, does anybody know what makes this book special? That's right, it is a library book. I don't own this book, do I? The library loaned this book to me, and eventually I will have to return it.

You know, life is kind of like that. We don't really own anything. Everything is loaned to us for a while. The land our church is on used to belong to other people, and someday we will all be gone and someone else will be worshipping here. Nothing we have lasts forever, does it? Except one thing--ourselves. Our minds, our hearts, our souls--what we are on the inside lives forever. That's what the Bible teaches us. Everything else is just loaned to us for a while. So we had better take care of our minds, our hearts, our souls, hadn't we? Because what we have inside of us lives forever.

KITE FLYING

Scripture Lesson: John 3:8

Object: A kite (or even a paper airplane if a kite is unavailable.)

Boys and girls, this is the month of March and in most places March is known for its wind. March is the month for getting out kites and flying them on the wind. How many of you have ever flown a kite before?

Now I want you to think for a moment about the wind that carries the kite up into the sky. You can't see the wind, can you? But you know it is there. Sometimes you can feel it — a cool breeze on a summer day or perhaps a cold wind in the winter time. Sometimes you can see what it is doing. You can watch it rustle the tree tops or carry your kite up hundreds of feet into the air. Sometimes the wind whirls in such a way that it becomes a tornado or a hurricane. Then you might see it turn over a car or even pick up a house. The wind can be very powerful and yet we cannot see the wind itself. We can only see things that move because of it.

Jesus had a hard time getting people to understand about God's spirit. He taught us that God is present with us — that he is at work in people's hearts helping them to become better people. Jesus wanted people to understand that God was with them even when they could not see him. So Jesus said that God's spirit is like the wind. He is present. He is working within people's lives even though we cannot see him.

Remember that if you fly your kite this week. As you watch the kite being lifted into the sky by a power you cannot see, remember that there is someone very close to you that you cannot see who loves you very much.

YOU LOOK JUST LIKE YOUR FATHER!

Scripture Lesson: Genesis 1:1; 2:3
Object: A mirror.

Boys and girls,

Some of you may have had somebody come up to you and say to you, "Why you look just like your father." Even tiny babies while they're in the hospital will have people peer through the window and say, "Why she's got her mother's eyes." "He looks exactly like his brother looked at that age." You've heard that, haven't you? Sometimes that happens even with children who are adopted. Because we love our parents so much, even when we are adopted, we may grow to look like them. In fact, they say that married couples – after they have lived together for a long time – start resembling each other. That is because, when we are very close to somebody – when we admire them a great deal – we begin to smile like they smile and walk like they walk. As we grow older, we often become like the persons we love in both our looks and in the way we act.

Usually that is good because our parents are fine people. But even if they were not good people, or even if we do not have parents, there is still hope for us. That is because the Bible tells us that we have another father besides our earthly father. Who is that? That's right, it's God. God is our Father. Wouldn't it be great if we could love God enough so that we could become like him. Wouldn't it be great if we could be just as loving, just as forgiving, just as kind as God is? Wouldn't it be great if people could say, "He's just like his Father?" This is Father's Day and most of us would like to be like our Dad. Let's try also to resemble our Heavenly Father as well.

SHARING YOUR EXCITEMENT

Scripture Lesson: Matthew 10:16-33
Object: A newspaper and a Bible.

Boys and girls:

I didn't bring my newspaper this morning in order to catch up on the sports or the business news or to read what "Dear Abby" has to say. I didn't even bring it to read Peanuts, Garfield or Family Circle. **(Substitute comic strips in your local paper.)** I brought it to help you think about good news.

Years ago, before there was television, newsboys would stand on the street corners selling newspapers. If something really special had happened in the news, they would yell, "Extra! Extra! Read all about it!" They wanted people to buy a newspaper to read the news.

The same kind of things happen on television today. You might be watching your favorite television program and the announcer might break in to say, "We bring you this special report from our news bureau in Washington." Of course, news in the papers or on radio or television is usually not good news, is it? Usually it is very bad news.

The Bible, on the other hand, is very good news. It is the story of God's love made known through Jesus Christ. Jesus wanted his disciples to go out and tell the world of God's love. We might imagine newspaper boys standing on street corners yelling, "Extra! Extra! Read all about it! God loves you!" But that might not be the best way to tell others. Perhaps simply inviting someone to visit your Sunday class would be a good way. Of course, the best way to tell others about God's love is to live the way God wants us to live. If others see God's love in our lives, that is the best witness of all.

SMALL BODY BUT A BIG HEART

Scripture Lesson: Luke 19:1-10

Boys and girls:

I love the story of Zaccheus, don't you? Zaccheus was a short, little man. He was so short that when the crowds came out to see Jesus, Zaccheus had to climb a tree to get a good view. I'll bet some of you have had that problem at some time or another, haven't you? Maybe it was at a parade. Maybe your father placed you on his shoulders so you could see over the adults.

That was the kind of problem that Zaccheus had. He was short, but he had an even bigger problem. He was a tax-collector. Now some of us adults may not like tax-collectors today. After all, they take our money and give it to the government. In Jesus' time, though, the tax-collectors did worse than that. They cheated people and took from them more than they owed the government, and then they kept the extra for themselves. That is why people hated tax-collectors. That was Zaccheus' biggest problem – not his little body but his stingy and evil heart.

Jesus changed all that. He went home with Zaccheus and had dinner with him. As they talked something happened to Zaccheus. Oh, he didn't grow any larger on the outside, but he did start to grow on the inside. And he made a promise to Jesus to give back four times what he had cheated people out of.

Jesus can help us do that too. He can help us grow big on the inside by filling us with His love.

BOY OR GIRL?

Scripture Lesson: John 4:5-42
Object: A pink ribbon and a blue ribbon; a doll and a football.

Boys and girls, I have two ribbons here. One color of ribbon we normally associate with girls? (**Let them answer.**) I'm curious. How many of you girls prefer pink over blue? I have two more objects with me – a doll and a football. Do you think of one as a girl's toy and the other as a boy's?

The first thing that was asked about you when you were born was whether you were a boy or a girl. Probably if you were a boy you were treated one way. If you were a girl you were treated another right from the beginning of your life. That's all right. Boys and girls are different. What is not all right is for us to think that one is better than the other.

When Jesus lived, people thought the boys were better than girls. They sold slaves back then. A boy baby could be bought for 5 shekels, a girl baby for only 3. That is because back then most people earned their living with their bodies as farmers or fishermen or soldiers. Boys would usually grow up to be bigger and stronger, so they were valued more. Women were generally looked down on.

Jesus knew that wasn't right. He knew that we are all God's children and God loves us just the same whether we are males or females. Jesus treated everybody equally. I believe he wants each of us to do the same. Some of you girls are dreaming of doing things that your mothers never did – becoming doctors, lawyers, and all kinds of things. God has given you a good mind. He wants you to use it. We are all God's children. He loves us all the same.

WHEN GOD GETS OUR ATTENTION

Scripture Lesson: Exodus 3:1-15
Object: A trick birthday candle that re-ignites after being blown out (available at almost any variety store).

If God wanted to get our attention, how would he go about it? I've brought a candle with me. Let me light it. We are all familiar with candles, aren't we? They make nice decorations at Christmas time and, of course, for birthdays. Here _____, would you blow the candle out for me **(let him or her blow the candle).** Perhaps you didn't blow hard enough. **(Let them try again.)** Some of you already know that this is a trick candle. No matter how hard you blow on it, it lights back up. I don't know how it works, but it is fascinating.

In our lesson from the Old Testament today God wanted to get Moses' attention. He didn't use a candle that wouldn't blow out, did he? What did he use? That's right, he used a bush that was on fire, but didn't burn up. He wanted to get Moses' attention — to tell him to go down into Egypt to rescue the children of Israel.

Usually God doesn't do tricks to get our attention. He doesn't tug on our arm like a friend might do to get our attention. He doesn't hold up his hand, like we may do when we want to get our teacher's attention. Usually God waits patiently for us to give him our attention. We give our attention to God when we bow our heads for prayer, when we study the Bible, when we listen to our Sunday School teacher or to the minister. God is speaking to us whenever we give him our attention. He is telling us about his love, and the way that is best for us to live. Let's give God our attention by bowing our heads for a moment in prayer. **(Lead the children in a closing prayer.)**

STICKS AND STONES

Scripture Lesson: John 8:1-11
Objects: A stick and a stone.

Can you imagine why I have this stick and this stone with me this morning? Does anyone know a poem with sticks and stones in it? That's right:

Sticks and stones will break my bones,
But words will not hurt me.

Have you ever heard that little poem? Now we know that sticks and stones can hurt us, don't we? In Jesus' time when someone had done something really wrong, they would sometimes stone them to death. Can you imagine having people throw rocks at you until they killed you? That would be awful. Have you ever thrown a rock at a dog or a cat or a bird? The next time you're about to do something like that, think about how awful it would be to have a stone thrown at you. We know that sticks and stones can hurt us.

Can words hurt us, though? Yes, they can. We usually say that someone "hurt our feelings." And our feelings can hurt just as much as our head or our arm or our leg. What are some things we can say to others that might hurt their feelings? That's right, we can say something about their looks, their size. We can say something about their clothes or the kind of car their family has. We can call them names. It is very easy to hurt someone else's feelings, isn't it?

Sometimes we have to ask ourselves, just like we ask about how it would feel if someone threw rocks at us, how would it feel if someone teased me about that? How would it feel if someone called me that? Would it hurt my feelings?

I don't believe any of us would want to hurt any other person with sticks or stones, or with words.

HE LOVES ME, HE LOVES ME NOT

Scripture Lesson: I Corinthians 13
Object: A flower from which you can pick petals, or an apple.

Boys and girls, have you ever taken a flower, especially a daisy, and pulled its petals off and said, "He loves me, he loves me not. She loves me, she loves me not." Now some of you boys would never admit that you have done that. Some of you would never admit that you even liked girls. That's perfectly normal. Some of you girls are not all that interested in boys either, and that's perfectly normal too. But we do have to admit that one of the fun parts of life is that there are girls and there are boys, and someday we are likely to fall in love with somebody else.

Another way of doing that is to take an apple and twist the stem, and as you twist the stem, say the alphabet – A, B, C, D, – and then when the stem breaks, that is the first letter of the name of the person you are going to marry. That's a silly superstition.

I know that you are aware that love plays a big role on television programs. Everyone is always in love with someone else. That's part of what makes the programs interesting. But some of us might not like those mushy love scenes on television, they are kind of yucky, aren't they? But one day they will mean more to us than they do now.

Love is very important in our lives. Love for a member of the opposite sex, and love within our families – this is what helps keep the world going. There is a little song that goes:

"It's love, it's love, it's love that makes the world go around.

"It's love, it's love, it's love that makes the world go around."

That's true. Life wouldn't be worth living if we were totally by ourselves. What makes life wonderful is knowing that people love us.

The Bible tells us that love doesn't just happen – that it comes from the heart of God. That is why I can love my wife, that is why your parents can love you. That is why we can love each other in this church — because God has placed in our world the gift of love — the most wonderful gift of all.

So the next time you are doing, "He loves me, he loves me not" with a flower, you remember that you don't have to ask that about God. It is not a matter of "He loves me, he loves me not." He always loves us. In fact, it is from him that love first came.

THE HAPPY GARDENER

Scripture Lesson: John 14:23-29
Object: A potted plant or flower.

(If you do any gardening yourself, a personal experience would be the best introduction to this children's sermon.)

As you may know, boys and girls, many parts of our country were very cold this past April. Even in the South where it is usually much warmer than the rest of the country there were many nights in April when the temperature fell below the freezing point. I'll bet there were some disappointed gardeners in those places.

Most people who like to plant flowers take real pride in their plants. They like to see beautiful flowers bloom forth after they have done the careful work of digging in the soil, fertilizing, watering. But a sudden freeze can kill your newly planted flowers. It is a big disappointment to go outside after a cold night and see your beautiful tulips with their heads drooping and your azaleas looking so wilted, when just a few days ago they had been looking so beautiful.

Don't you imagine that is how God feels when he sees some of his children not growing like He intended? A happy gardener has flowers that are growing and blossoming just as he intended. God is happy, the Bible tells us, when his children are happy and healthy and loving and doing the things He created them to do. Jesus said that we show our love for God by obedience. Obedience means simply that we become what God means for us to become — a person who in many ways is like Jesus himself. He was loving and kind and good. Let's make God happy by being loving and kind and good too.

CHRIST THE KING

Scripture Lesson: Luke 23:35-43
Object: Pictures of world rulers if you can find them, or some symbol of power; or make a crown.

Would one of you describe what a king looks like? **(Give a few of them a chance to describe their mental image of a king.)** What does a king do. How would you describe a king? Would you like to be a king or a queen? Usually when we think of a king, we think of someone very powerful, don't we? We think of someone with a crown on his head. We think of other people bowing down before the king and doing everything that the king demands. Some of the kings in today's world don't wear robes and crowns, though. They wear business suits or soldier's uniforms. They may also wear all kinds of medals and insignias and perhaps a special sash at formal celebrations. Most of them are still very powerful, and some of them are very cruel.

Suppose you saw someone in a garden with very simple clothing on, though, and he was kneeling on the ground praying. As you looked closer, you could see that he was deeply troubled. Perspiration was rolling off his forehead. And you heard him pray, "Father, if it be possible, let this cup pass from me. . . ." Would you guess that this man was a king? Probably not, but that is how we remember the King of Kings — kneeling in a garden, riding on a donkey, being born in a manger. For who is this King of Kings? Of course, it is Jesus. He showed us that greatness comes not from having a crown, or a sash, or a great high throne. Greatness comes from having the love of God in our hearts.

FOR ALL PEOPLE

Scripture Lesson: Isaiah 56:1-8;
                       Matthew 15:21-28
Object: An admission ticket.

Boys and girls,

What if you were going to McDonald's or Burger King or wherever you like to eat and saw a sign that said, "Black people only"? And you watched lots of other boys and girls going in and eating and having a good time, but you could not go in because your skin was white. You would feel bad, wouldn't you?

I can remember when that used to be true in certain parts of our country. White people could go into nice restaurants, but people with dark skin could not. That's silly, isn't it? But that's the way it was. I was reading about a man many years ago named Otto Kahn who gave more than 2 million dollars to the Metropolitan Opera, but Mr. Kahn was not allowed to be a boxholder at the opera because Mr. Kahn was Jewish. He had given them over 2 million dollars, but he couldn't get a box seat because of his religion. That's hard to believe, but I understand it is true.

That's called prejudice, isn't it? And quite often different groups in our country have been the victims of prejudice — blacks, Jews, Mexican Americans, persons of Oriental ancestry, Native Americans, which we call Indians, etc. People who are prejudiced forget that the Bible says that we all come from one mother and father — Adam and Eve. We are all part of God's family. "Jesus loves the little children, all the children of the world."

I'm glad we don't have to have tickets like this one to come to church. Tickets let us in places, but they also keep people out of places if they don't have one. This church is for all people. We would never want anybody to feel that they could not come in. This is a house of prayer for all people.

KEYS TO THE KINGDOM

Scripture Lesson: Matthew 16:13-20
Object: A set of keys.

Boys and girls,

Last week we had a ticket as our object. This week we have a set of keys. You may remember that last week in talking about tickets, we said that a ticket can get you into a movie or an amusement park or somewhere else, but tickets can also keep you out — if you don't have one.

Now what do keys do? That's right, they let people get into locked doors. In our Scripture lesson today Jesus gives to Simon Peter the keys of the Kingdom. Jesus was starting the Christian church and he was starting with Simon Peter. Jesus was giving Peter and his whole church the keys to the Kingdom of God.

Now there are several ways of looking at this. We might imagine the Kingdom of God as Heaven — that beautiful place where people go when they die. You may have seen pictures in cartoons of St. Peter standing there with his keys letting people into heaven. That's one way of looking at it.

But there are others. I believe that the church of Jesus Christ has the key to being happy right here in this world. I believe the church has the key to understanding what life is about. I believe we have the key to what God is like. These are keys (**hold up the keys**), that only the church of Jesus Christ has. People come here to learn about God. They come here to meet people who know how to truly love them. They come here to put their lives back together again. We have the keys. The church has the keys. In fact, we believe that Jesus Christ is the key to life and love and truth in this world and in heaven.

A YOUNG BOY TO THE RESCUE

Scripture Lesson: Matthew 14:13-21
Object: Some loose change.

Boys and girls,

You know this story almost as well as I do, don't you? There were 5,000 people that Jesus needed to feed, but he had no food. How much food did he have? That's right, he had five loaves of bread and two small fish. What did the boy do with them? That's right. He gave them to Jesus. Jesus blessed the five loaves and two fish and somehow he was able to feed 5,000 people. It is a great story, isn't it?

I want you to imagine that you have some change in your pocket, O.K.? Perhaps you have some quarters and nickels and dimes and maybe even a half dollar.

Now suppose you were to give that little bit of change to Jesus through our church. It doesn't seem like much — just a little bit of change — not even enough to buy an ice cream cone in some places. But you give it to Jesus. And suppose other boys and girls do the same thing.

Now imagine somewhere in Asia or Africa there are people who don't have enough food to eat to keep them alive. Only a dollar or so each day would buy them enough food, but they don't even have a dollar. But back in America these boys and girls are giving their change to Jesus and their parents are doing the same thing and, lo and behold, when you combine their nickels and quarters and dollars, soon there is enough money to feed thousands and thousands of people. Did you know that that miracle is happening every day? That little bit of change given to Jesus by boys and girls like you and like your parents is feeding thousands of people around the world. When we put money in the offering plate, we are like that little boy offering his five loaves and two tiny fish. It doesn't seem like we are doing much, but God can do great things with everything we give him.

WOW! A MIRACLE!

Scripture Lesson: Matthew 14:22-23
Object: A portable radio.

Boys and girls, today we read from the Bible of the time Jesus walked on the water. Wow! That must have been some miracle, don't you think? I can swim, I can float. But if I were to try to walk on the water I would probably drown, wouldn't I?

I brought with me this morning my radio. **(If you are adventurous, turn it on for a moment.)** A radio doesn't seem like much of a miracle to you and me. But to people born back in our great grandparent's time, it would be. They didn't have radios or televisions. The idea that a man in Washington, D.C. could be talking and that his voice could come out of this box thousands of miles away would have been unbelievable to them. It would seem like a miracle.

In your lifetime, you will see many miracles. You will see many things that you wouldn't have believed possible, but they will still happen. We live in a fantastic world. Behind that world is the mind of God, and there is no limit to the wonderful things God can do. God has also given us good minds, and there's almost no limit to what can come from a human mind. One of you might one day be an inventor of something that everybody else said was impossible. That's why we go to school and come to church — to let our minds grow — to learn how, with God's help, we can help perform miracles in the world. Only Jesus could walk on water, but one day with God's help many of you might do things that seem just as miraculous.

PLAYING HOUSE

Scripture Lesson: I Corinthians 7:32-35
Object: A teacup and a bar of soap (Ivory, if possible).

Boys and girls,

This morning in the sermon I am going to talk about marriage. I don't guess any of you are married, are you? Of course not. You are a little young. I imagine that you have "played house" some time or another, haven't you? You might have gotten a toy tea set and said, "Now you be the father and I will be the mother."

It's great to have families. Sometimes it's hard, too. You may fight with your brothers and sisters or even argue with your parents. Your mother and father may argue or they may even be divorced. That's hard. We are human beings and human beings sometimes get angry with one another. But part of being a family is that we keep trying to love one another even when we are angry.

I have a bar of soap with me, but it is not just an ordinary bar. It is a bar of Ivory soap. Do you know what is special about Ivory soap? That's right. It floats. I read once about how it happened that Ivory soap was first made. A little over 100 years ago a worker at a small soap factory forgot to turn off his machine while he went to lunch. This produced this frothing mass of lather filled with air bubbles. He almost threw it away, but he made it into soap anyway. Lo and behold, he discovered that the soap he made floated. This was very important because this was long before people had indoor plumbing. Some people still bathed in rivers and lakes. With Ivory they didn't have to worry about losing their soap in the water. Ivory was a big success, but it started out as a big mistake.

Everybody makes mistakes. Not all of them turn out as successfully as did Ivory. In our families we make mistakes. We make mistakes. Our brothers and sisters make mistakes. Our parents make mistakes. But we don't give up. We keep loving each other and trying to make one another happy. And with God's help, it works. Playing house becomes lots of fun.

THE MIRACLE OF HEALING

Scripture Lesson: Mark 1:29-39
Object: A band-aid and some mercurochrome or other medicine for minor cuts.

Boys and girls,

I am constantly amazed at the miraculous world in which we live. Our lesson from the Bible is about one of the miracles Jesus performed — a miracle of healing. All of us are thrilled to hear about somebody who was very sick and miraculously was healed. Have you ever thought about how wonderfully made we are so that our bodies can be healed?

Have you ever cut your finger or some other part of your body? I'll bet you have. It's not a very pleasant thought, but suppose I am peeling an apple and I cut my finger. It starts to bleed.

It is a scary thing to have a cut and to bleed, but I put some medicine on it. The medicine won't heal the cut, but it will keep germs from causing an infection. Then what do I do? That's right, I might put a band-aid on it. The band-aid won't heal the cut either, but it might stop the bleeding, and it might keep us from hurting it again while healing is taking place.

Now the medicine did not heal the cut and the band-aid did not heal the cut. Where did the healing come from? It comes from within the body itself. God has made us in a wonderful way so that our bodies have great healing powers.

Now even more amazing to me is that doctors have discovered that our thoughts and feelings can help or hurt the body heal faster. A person with good thoughts and good feelings will heal easier than a person who is frightened or angry or resentful. Maybe that is how Jesus healed people. He helped them relax and believe in God so that their bodies would heal themselves.

I don't know if that is the way it worked or not. But I do know that we are never too young to start thinking good thoughts. Loving Jesus and loving other people is a great way to learn and to have good thoughts and good feelings. Learning to share and learning to have fun with others are excellent ways to be healthy on the inside and on the outside as well.

IS YOUR LIGHT SHINING

Scripture Lesson: II Corinthians 4:3-6
Object: A lantern if at all possible, but a flashlight will do.

Boys and girls,

There is an old story about a terrible train wreck. After the wreck there was a trial to see who was at fault when the wreck occurred. On the witness stand was an old gentleman who was the watchman at the crossing where the wreck occurred. He was very nervous on the witness stand as the prosecuting attorney asked him, "Were you at the crossing on the night that the crash occurred?" "Yes," he answered, "I was." "Did you see the train coming and know that the other train was still stopped a little farther down the track?" The watchman was very nervous. He fidgeted and answered, "Yes, I did." Finally the prosecutor asked very solemnly, "Did you wave your lantern to tell the engineer of the train to stop?" The watchman was sweating profusely, but he finally blurted out his answer, "Yes, I waved my lantern."

They let him off of the witness stand, after all he had waved his lantern just like he was supposed to do. "Yes," he said, "I waved my lantern. But I was afraid they would ask me if my lantern was lit."

The watchman had been late getting to the crossing and had not lit his lantern. He had waved it frantically, but what good is a lantern that is not lit?

Many times we have talked about letting our light shine. We are to show the whole world the love of Jesus. Some people, however, have a hard time sharing Jesus' love because they have never opened their hearts to receive Jesus' love. Their lives are like a lantern that has never been lit. Sometimes it is good for us to pray, "Lord Jesus, help me to know your love in order that I may love others more. Shine your light into my life so that I can shine for others."

YOU HAVE ALREADY WON!

Scripture Lesson: Genesis 9:8-15
I Peter 3:18-22
Object: A letter (if possible, a sweepstakes letter, i.e., Publisher's Clearing House), and a Bible.

Boys and girls,

We all like to win something, don't we? We like to win at games and sports. We particularly like to receive a prize when we win. A lot of mail order promotions feature enormous prizes – boats, cars, houses. You have probably seen commercials that say, "I would like to give you one million dollars . . . "

My favorite letters, however, are those that start off, "You may have already won $50,000 . . . ." They are telling me that a number has been drawn that may be my number. All I have to do is write back to find out. But the drawing has already taken place. The contest is over. I may have already won.

Actually I have never won a contest in my life – well, except one. The Bible tells me that I won one contest before I was even born. Jesus won it for me. I don't understand exactly how he did it, but when Jesus died on the cross 2,000 years ago, he made it possible for you and me to win the greatest prize of all – eternal life. The Bible is kind of a letter from God saying, "You have already won. All you have to do is claim your prize. It's yours. All you have to do is accept it."

That's a very deep idea for most of us, but I am thankful for Jesus, aren't you? I am thankful for his love for me, and for you, and for the whole world. Because he has made it possible for all of us to be winners.

A FLASHLIGHT OR A LANTERN?

Scripture Lesson: Isaiah 60:1-6
Objects: A flashlight and a lantern (a lamp will do).

Boys and girls,

I have two kinds of light here. What are they? That's right, a flashlight and a lantern. **(Light the lantern and turn on the flashlight.)** Both of these give light, don't they? But there are several ways they are different. Can you think of some ways? That's right − one you light with a match and one you turn on using batteries. One has more glass than the other. One smokes and the other doesn't.

That's very good. I want to ask you another question. If you wanted a light to light your room, which would you want − the lantern or the flashlight? Probably you would want the lantern. Why? That's right, the lantern spreads light throughout the room, doesn't it? But suppose on a dark night you heard a noise in your backyard, and you wanted to see what was out there without having to go outdoors, which would you want? That's right, you would probably want the flashlight. A flashlight focuses its light so that the light can extend a long way. It's not very good for lighting a room, but it is good for seeing a long way off.

There are many kinds of light, including the sun and the candles on our altar. There are floodlights, and street lights, and Christmas tree lights and all kinds of lights. But do you know the little song, "This little light of mine, I'm gonna let it shine . . .?" It reminds me of our lesson from Isaiah when he says, "Arise, Shine for your light has come . . . " The Bible teaches us that Jesus is the light of the world, but it also teaches us that each of us is a light. When we let God's love shine through us, we can be like a lantern filling up a whole room with God's love or like a flashlight − focusing God's love on somebody far away. The main thing is to let our light shine.

A REAL SUPERSTAR

Scripture Lesson: Mark 1: 4-11

Object: A fan magazine or a baseball glove endorsed by a pro, or any object to help the children think about "stars" in entertainment or sports.

Boys and girls,

I'll bet everybody here has their favorite movie star, or singer or ball player. I have some favorites. **(Name some of them and have the children name some.)** I'll bet you have seen some very famous people on television on commercials.

I understand that when Jimmy Connors, the famous tennis player, makes a commercial, he gets paid $50,000 for just a one-minute commercial on television. The great boxer Muhammad Ali gets paid as much as $200,000 — not for boxing but just for showing his pretty face on television for sixty seconds. Actor James Coburn, we are told, once got paid one-half million dollars for just saying two words on a beer commercial.

Movie stars and famous athletes make lots of money, but the most famous person who ever lived never got paid a dime. I mean there once lived a man who has had millions of books written about him. Millions of songs have been written about him. Nearly one billion people celebrate his birthday every year. But he never made a dime for it. In fact, he ended up on a cross, dying between two thieves. Who am I talking about? That's right, Jesus Christ. He received no earthly reward for his fame. But he did receive something else. He received the satisfaction of knowing that he had showed you and me just how much God loves us. Here we are in our church 2,000 years later, and we are still talking about God's love because of what Jesus did. Other stars have come and gone — and some of them were well paid — but all will someday die and be forgotten. But the name of Jesus will thrill persons of all ages in every age as long as there are people upon this earth.

FREAKY FRIDAY—SENSATIONAL SUNDAY

Scripture Lesson: Matthew 11:25-30
Object: A baby's rattle.

Boys and girls,

Have any of you ever seen a Walt Disney movie by the name of *Freaky Friday*? *Freaky Friday* was a silly movie about a mother and her teenaged daughter who changed places for a while. The mother had the daughter's mind and the daughter had her mother's mind. Can you imagine your mother acting like a teen-ager? Chewing bubble gum and turning the radio real loud and throwing her clothes all over the house and talking on the phone all the time, etc. Now let me hasten to say that none of the teenagers in our church act like that, but I have heard of some who do.

How would you like to trade places with your parents for a week? You would go to work and they would go to school and sit in your desk. That's funny. Suppose I stood up on Sunday morning before my sermon and shook this baby rattle. You would wonder what was wrong with me.

And yet there are a couple of times in the Bible when Jesus told grown ups that they need to become like little children, and in today's lesson, like babes.

At first that sounds silly, doesn't it? Can you imagine me in a baby buggy? And yet think how trusting a little baby is. And how loving. A little baby trusts its parents to provide his or her needs. I'll bet that babies and very small children don't worry very much. They know they will be taken care of. You know that too, don't you? God loves you and He will always provide for you. You trust Him, don't you? I wish all of our grownups could trust Him like you do.

DO IT FOR JESUS

Scripture Lesson: Matthew 10:37-42
Object: A cup of cold water.

Boys and girls,

I have here a cup of cold water. If I offered you a drink of water, you would probably take it if you were thirsty. If it were a Coke or a Sprite or some other soft drink that you really like, you might take it even if you were not thirsty.

You know that you cannot live very long without water, don't you? Even if you went only a few days without liquid, you would be in trouble. In parts of our country where there are deserts, water is especially important, isn't it? In the old west the cowboys would fight range wars over water for their cattle. If you had a stream going through your ranch, you were particularly fortunate. In fact, the word "Rivalry" — have you heard that word before? — is a kind of a fight. It comes from the Latin word, **Rivus** which means a stream. Wars have been fought over water. Water is so precious.

In the land in which Jesus lived, it was hot and dry. One of the nicest things you could do for people was to give them a cup of cold water. Jesus said that it was so nice that whenever you gave someone else a cup of cold water in his name it was as though you were really giving it to Jesus. Whenever we do something nice for someone — whether its our friend or our teacher or our brother or sister or whoever it might be — we are doing it for Jesus. That's a nice thought. Do something nice for somebody today. Do it for Jesus!

DIFFERENT STROKES FOR DIFFERENT FOLKS

Scripture Lesson: Matthew 13:1-17
Object: A packet of seeds.

Boys and girls,

One of the things that the Bible never explains is why people are so different. Some people like chocolate ice cream. Others like strawberry. Some people like rock music. Some like country. Some like football. Others like baseball. Some people smile a lot. Others hardly smile at all. Some people are kind — even as tiny children. Others seem to be mean from the day they were born.

Jesus talked about how different people are. He talked about it in a parable. He said a man was sowing some grass seed. Some of the seeds fell on the path and the birds came along and devoured them. Some of the seeds fell on a rocky soil. They sprouted a little but never really grew very much. Others of the seed fell among the weeds and thorns and they were choked before they even had a chance. But some of the seed fell on good fertile soil, and it grew and multiplied and produced a great harvest.

Jesus was saying that people are like that. Some are like a path, some are like rocky soil, some are like the soil filled with weeds, and then some are like the rich, fertile soil. Of course, the seed was his teachings. He knew that some people would accept his teachings and some would not.

We don't know why people are so different. Perhaps we are born different. Maybe its because our parents treated us differently. We just don't know. Why are some people athletic and others are not? Why are some of us talkative and others shy? The important thing, however, is that we are all of equal value to God. He understands why we are like we are. And He loves us just as we are — even if we happen to be a little different.

A NUT LIKE YOU

Scripture Lesson: Matthew 13:24-35
Object: An acorn and a picture of a large tree.

Boys and girls,
I once heard a silly poem that went something like this:

Don't worry if your troubles be many
and your rewards be few;
Remember that mighty oak
was once a nut like you.

That's silly isn't it? But it is quite a thought to realize that a giant oak tree came from a tiny acorn like this one. That is the miracle of growth.

Have you ever seen a giant sequoia tree? Some of the sequoias get so large that it would take several of us holding hands to reach all the way around one. And yet the seeds that grow into giant sequoias are so small that it takes 3,000 of them to weigh one ounce. That is tiny. That is the miracle of growth. Of course, you know about the miracle of growth because you're growing, aren't you? You can look at us adults and see how big you will be in just a few years. That is the miracle of growth.

Jesus said that God's kingdom grows like a tiny seed. It started with a tiny babe in Bethlehem. Then there were twelve disciples. Soon there were thousands of people who were following Jesus. And today there are millions of persons in nearly every country in the world who know about God's love. That's a miracle. And every time we invite someone else to come with us to Sunday School or church, we are part of that miracle. When we help God's church to grow, we are part of one of the greatest miracles in the world.

ICE STATUES

Object: Picture of a snowman.

Boys and Girls:

Do you like to make snowmen? Or snowwomen? Or snow animals? Every year in Canada a Winter Carnival is held. The people have a contest to see who can make the best ice statue. In order to make ice statues, first of all, you make a big pile of snow and then sprinkle it with water. When your big pile of snow has turned to ice, you're ready to carve it. Using a small axe you can carve the ice into whatever shape you want it to be. It might be a bear, or an airplane, or a train. If you were making an ice statue, in what shape would you make it? (**Wait for answers.**)

You and I carve out snowmen and snowwomen each day in our lives in the things we do, and in the things we say, and even in the things we don't do and say. Our Bible tells us that "as a man thinketh in his heart, so is he." That means that we become the kind of person we are by what we do and say and think. If we do things that are good and right and loving, we are carving beautiful snow people. If we do things that are mean and ugly, then we carve out distorted and dreadful snow people.

What kind of ice statue will you carve today? I hope it will be the most beautiful statue ever created — a statue made of concern, kindness, courtesy, and love.

A POLAR BEAR'S SECRET

Object: A stuffed bear.

Boys and Girls:

I read something this week that I didn't know before. I was reading about polar bears — those gigantic white animals that live in the northern-most part of our continent — making their home in the ice and snow of the arctic region. These beautiful and ferocious animals are a wondrous part of God's creation.

The thing I learned about polar bears was this: Polar bears have hair on the bottom of their feet. Now that might sound silly to you — to have hair on the bottom of your feet. But it is not silly to polar bears. That hair serves as a kind of shoe for the polar bear allowing him to climb over the ice and snow. He would be a helpless creature without that hair.

God has adapted every creature for its own particular habitat. That is part of God's plan. You are part of God's plan too. He wants you to live happily and to enjoy this world in which He has placed you as His own child!

A BILL FROM GOD

Object: A bill (e.g., from a department store)

What am I holding in my hands this morning, boys and girls? Yes, a letter — but this is a very special kind of letter. That's right — it is a bill. If you see your mothers and fathers with a painful look on their faces, it is because they know all about bills. What is a bill? (**Give them an opportunity to answer.**) A bill means I bought something at a department store and now I have to pay for it. It is nice to buy new things, but sometimes it is hard to pay all the bills.

Just think — aren't you glad that God doesn't send us bills? What if you went to the mailbox and there was a bill from God for the sunshine? How much do you think sunshine is worth? Why, we couldn't live without it, could we? So I imagine it would be pretty expensive. What about rain? We may not always like rain, but if we didn't have it, how could we grow our food? What would we have to drink?

What if we had to pay God for our families or our friends? Wow, we would run out of money in a hurry, wouldn't we? What if we had to pay him for these wonderful bodies He has given us, or our brains? God has been so good to us. Look at how much he has so freely given us. Of course, the greatest gift He has given us is the gift of His own son. Jesus Christ is God's free gift to us. Now He wants us to share His free gift with others. He wants us to share joy and love and laughter with all our friends. If we will do that, he will be repaid.

HEARING GOD SPEAK

Object: A portable radio.

I am holding in my hand one of the most amazing inventions in man's history — what is it? That's right, it is a portable radio. A man can speak into a microphone miles away, or he can play a record, and I can hear it. I don't even have to pull a long extension cord behind me, do I? That's because this radio has a what in it? That's right — a battery.

Nowadays portable radios come in all kinds of shapes and sizes, don't they? Do any of you have a radio at home that's hidden inside a toy animal or perhaps a race car? **(Give them a chance for input.)** One of the most fascinating new developments are these portable radios that are built into a set of earphones. You might see someone walking along with a set of earphones that aren't attached to anything. That is because the radio is built in.

Wouldn't it be great to have a built-in radio that would pick up God's voice? That would make life so much easier. We would never make a mistake, would we? If we had a radio that would pick up God's voice, we could just turn on the radio whenever we had a big decision to make and He would guide us. Unfortunately, life isn't quite that simple. We don't have a built-in radio. That is why God gave us parents and Sunday School teachers. That is why God gave us the Bible — to help us hear His voice and to know his will for our lives.

PUNISHED FOR DOING GOOD

Scripture Lesson: I Peter 2:19-25
Object: A "switch" or a belt or some other traditional instrument for punishing children. (If your parents punished you physically as a child, the children will enjoy your sharing your experience. Do this with care. We do not want to encourage parents who could conceivably be abusive.)

Boys and girls,

I am not going to ask you if you have ever been spanked. Some parents believe in spanking children when they do wrong, others do not. Parents used to be stricter with their children than most parents are now. Your father or your grandfather might tell you that his parent took his belt off and whipped him, or a "switch" off of a tree limb or even a hair brush. At school it was not unusual for a teacher to swat a pupil with a ruler for doing wrong. Personally I am glad those days are gone, aren't you? Actually a parent's hand is plenty sufficient if a spanking must be administered.

Nobody likes to be punished, either with a spanking or not being allowed to watch television or whatever the punishment may be. But usually we understand when we have done wrong we will be punished. But what if you were punished for doing right? Did you know that some people are punished for doing right? Some people are punished even today for going to church or telling their neighbors about God or even being a friend to someone in trouble. It's one thing to be punished when you are wrong, but it would be bad to be punished for doing what you think is right. That happens to people, though. That happened to Jesus. He was crucified on the cross for doing what God wanted him to do. Let's give God thanks that in our country we are free to do what we think is right.

GOD'S LOVE IS LIKE A BABY BOTTLE

Scripture Lesson: I Peter 2:1-10
Object: A baby bottle.

Boys and girls,

I like the way the *Living Bible* translates I Peter 2:3, "Long to grow up into the fullness of your salvation; cry for this as a baby cries for his milk." Have you ever heard a baby cry? I don't mean a soft little moan. I mean a loud WA—A—A! Now a baby is not being mean when it cries, is it? A baby can't live without its milk just like you and I can't live without hamburgers or french fries or pizzas. A baby is helpless, isn't it? The only way a baby can tell the world that it needs to be fed is to cry. So when a baby cries it is saying to the world, "Help, I've got to have food or I will die."

The writer of our Scripture lesson is telling us just as that baby needs milk, you and I need the love of God in our hearts. We can't really live until that love comes into our heart. Oh, we may walk and talk. Our hearts may beat, and we may jump and run and play. But we really do not know how beautiful the world is until the love of God comes into our hearts.

How do we have that love? All we have to do is ask for it. "God, please send your love into my heart."

Now, you and I don't use a baby bottle anymore. We use knives and forks, and we can drink out of a glass. But we still need to eat and drink, don't we? You never outgrow your need for food. You never outgrow your need for God's love either. We need to long for it as a baby longs for its bottle.

OF DOVES AND WATER

Scripture Lesson: Luke 3:15-17, 21-22
Object: Picture of a dove.

There are two places in the Bible where a dove plays a very important role. Would you like to try and guess where those two places are? That's right, after the great flood Noah sent out a dove to find dry land. Then in our lesson for the morning, the Holy Spirit comes upon Jesus in the form of a dove. There is another element that is in both stories. What element is that? That's right, *water.* In the story of Noah water is used to destroy man. In the story of Jesus' baptism, water is the symbol, not of destroying man but of saving man.

We can drown in water — or we can take a bath and use water to make us clean. Of course, Jesus isn't so concerned that our bodies are as clean as much as he wants our hearts to be clean. He wants us to have kind and loving hearts. He wants us to think about and do those things that we know are right.

Of course, baptism is important for another reason. By baptism we join God's family. Our baptism symbolizes the fact that we are a follower of Jesus. We may not see a dove when we are baptized. But we can know that God's spirit is with us and that we are His own children.

A PERSONAL CALL

Scripture Lesson: I Samuel 3:1-20
Object: A toy telephone.

It's exciting to get a telephone call, isn't it? "It's for you," your Mom calls out. Those are good words to hear. Somebody cares enough about us to give us a personal call.

There is a beautiful story in the Bible that some of you have already heard in Sunday School. It is about a young man named Samuel who was awakened one night by someone calling his name. It wasn't a telephone call. They didn't have telephones back then. All he heard was a voice. He thought it was the prophet Eli — for he was living with the prophet at that time. He went to Eli's room. But Eli told him that it was not he who had called. Samuel lay back down. But again he hears the voice calling. Again he went to Eli's room, but it was not Eli calling him. Finally Eli realized that it was God calling Samuel. "Go back." he told Samuel, "and when you hear the voice say, "Speak Lord, your servant hears.' Samuel does go back to his room. Then the Lord calls his name again. This time Samuel speaks the words Eli told him and God begins to tell Samuel His purpose for him. God speaks directly to Samuel. No telephone — no radio — just a voice in the night.

Has God ever spoken to you? I doubt that He has ever called you on the telephone. I doubt that many of us have ever heard Him speak our name at night. For most of us, God speaks to us silently through our own minds. He helps us to know right from wrong. He gives us courage when we are afraid. He helps us in school. Oh, He doesn't magically flash the answers to a test on the blackboard so that only we can see. God isn't a genie in a bottle. But if we have studied our homework, He can help us keep our cool so that we always do our best. Even if we never hear Him speak in a voice that we can hear with our physical ears, we can know that He is with us. We can know that because we know He loves us and He has promised that He will always be with us.

WHAT KIND OF CLOCKS IN HEAVEN?

Scripture Lesson: Luke 21:5-19
Objects: A bag full of different time pieces, if attainable. If not, just one clock.

Boys and girls:

How many different kinds of clocks do you guess there are? Can you think of some? Grandfather clocks — cuckoo clocks — wind-up clocks that go tick-tick — electric clocks — alarm clocks — pocket watches — digital watches — stop watches — watches that chime on the hour. We could go on all morning just naming the different kinds of clocks. Some we hang on our walls at homes. Some giant ones we might see on the side of banks. Others are so small that we can wear them on our wrists. All of them have one job, though. What is that? All of them measure time.

A clock or a watch tells us how much time has gone by. I am 30 minutes older than I was when our worship service started. And so are you. I will be three hours older when the football game starts this afternoon on television than I am right now. Clocks measure time.

What kind of clocks do you guess we will find in heaven? Will they be giant clocks? Will they all be made out of gold? What kind of clock do you think God has? Now I don't know this for sure, but I suspect that God doesn't own a watch. And I kind of suspect that there are no clocks in heaven — even giant, gold ones. That is because no one ever grows old in heaven. No one ever dies. Every day lasts forever. Night never comes. That's hard for us to imagine, isn't it? But the Bible teaches us that one day this world will be taken away, and a new perfect world will replace it. I don't know exactly what that world will be like, but I know this: God is the best friend we have. If He's going to replace this world some day with a new world, it will be a great place to live.

FOR SPECIAL OCCASIONS

Object: A silver teaspoon and a stainless steel tea spoon.

Boys and girls, what am I holding? That's right — two spoons. Now let me have a volunteer. (**Have one of the children hold both spoons.**) Do you notice any difference between the two spoons? That's right — one of the spoons is heavier than the other.

Now what do you think is the difference between the two spoons that makes one heavier than the other? One spoon is made out of . . . (**Give them an opportunity to answer.**) silver, and the other is made of stainless steel. Which of the two is more expensive. That's right — the silver spoon.

We all know that in the past year the price of both silver and gold went very, very high. In fact, the price of silver has gone so high than many families are putting their silver in safety deposit boxes at the bank, and taking it out only for special occasions. A set of silver is now so expensive and so easy for burglars to carry off, so many families are putting their silver where they can reach it only for special occasions.

Some people do the same thing to God. They believe in God. They are glad that God exists. But they only turn to Him on special occasions. Like Easter, or Christmas, or when somebody they love is very sick. The rest of the time they forget about God. That is a shame.

The more often we turn to God, the more help we find Him to be. In fact, those persons who walk with Him each day discover that He is the best friend they have.

STAYING POWER

Scripture Lesson: John 12:20-33
Object: A pair of running shoes.

Boys and girls,

I read the most fascinating bit of information this week that I want to share with you. All of you know what these are, don't you? That's right, these are running shoes. Lot's of people are taking up running. It's a great sport. But I want to ask you a question. I want to ask you if you can out run certain animals.

Let's begin with a cheetah. Do you know what a cheetah is? That's right. It is the fastest animal around. It can run 70 miles an hour. How would you do in a race with a cheetah? How about a race horse? Well, how about a timber wolf? How would you do in a race with each of these animals? You think you would lose. Well, in a short race you would. But did you know that in a race that is long enough, you would win? Animals have hearts and lungs that allow them to run very fast in short spurts. But then they have to rest. The human body, however, is the most efficient running machine on earth. If you are in good health and in good condition, your body can run farther than any animal can match. You can keep running long after they have all tired out. God has given you a wonderful body with great staying power. But it has to be in good condition.

Of course, some people give up in life even though they have good bodies. They become discouraged. They get down on themselves. They let their unhappiness cause them to quit trying. That's not because something is wrong with their bodies but with their minds, with their souls.

It is even more important that we keep our minds and souls in good condition than our body. One way we do that is to worship God. When we worship God we condition our spiritual hearts just like running helps our physical hearts.

I DON'T HAVE TIME

Scripture Lessons: Ecclesiastes 3:1
Object: A calendar.

Sometimes your parents are heard to say these very familiar words, "I do not have time." Maybe you need something fixed and you go to them, but they are busy with something else. "I do not have time right now," they say. Perhaps you want your dad to play ball with you. "Maybe tomorrow," he says, "I just don't have time today."

Of course, sometimes we are the ones who don't have time. All of us get busy with projects that we need to finish. We don't want to leave those projects unfinished, so we say, "I don't have time."

What do I have in my hands? It's a calendar, isn't it? The calendar is divided into what? That's right, months and weeks and days. Did you realize that all of us have the same amount of time? We all have how many hours in a day? That's right, 24. And how many days in a week? That's right, 7. And how many months in a year? That's right, 12.

We all have the same amount of time in a day. It is how we use our time that tells if we are wise or not. If we get so busy that we do not have time for sufficient rest or work or play or time with our family or friends or the other important things in our lives, then we have not made wise use of our time. If we do not have time for the really important matters in our lives, then maybe we need to make some changes.

ETERNAL VALUES

Scripture Lesson: Hebrews 1
Object: A yardstick and a Bible.

Boys and girls:

What do I have in my hand? Of course, it's a yardstick. What do you do with a yardstick? That's right, you measure things with it. Suppose we didn't have yardsticks or rulers, what would we do? Suppose your mother sent you to buy some material at a store. She wanted you to buy three yards of material. But suppose the salesperson had no ruler? Do you know how they used to do it before they had rulers? The salesperson would pull the material out one arm's length and cut if off. Now what was wrong with that? Of course, what if the salesperson had short arms? Then you wouldn't get very much material. Or what if the salesperson had very long arms? You might get a bargain. Or suppose you wanted to measure off a football field. In the old days, they might have measured it off in feet. Oh, I don't mean feet like on a yardstick. They might have lined up 300 men's shoes and that would be one hundred yards for a football field. But what if some of the men had big feet? A punt-returner might have had to run a long way to make a touchdown. No, we need some things in this world that never change. We need to know that a yard will always be the same distance. We need to know that a foot is twelve inches regardless of how big men's feet get.

That is another reason we need the Bible. It helps us know that some things never change — like truth, and goodness, and God's love for His children.

LESSON FROM A RAISIN CAKE

Scripture Lesson: Job 38:1-11; 16-18
Object: A raisin cake.

Have you ever watched some children eat raisin cakes — those little packaged cakes that you buy at the store that have raisins on them? A certain little girl loved cake, but did not like raisins. So every time her mother bought raisin cakes, the little girl would take them off to a secret place and carefully remove each of the raisins. Some of you might do the same thing. And yet raisins are much better for you than cake. Raisins contain iron that your body needs.

Some people want to live their lives like that. They want to eat cake all the time, but never want to eat the raisins. They want to do only those things that they enjoy — never the things that are good for them. Some children come to Sunday School and want to play the entire time and not study. That's perfectly natural, but if we want to grow to be the kind of person God wants us to be, we soon learn that there is a time for play and a time for study. There is a time for enjoying ourselves and there is a time for bringing joy to others. There is a time for cake, but also for raisins.

BACKBONES, LAZY BONES, DRY BONES

Scripture Lesson: Ezekiel 37:1-14
Object: A bone.

Boys and girls,

I brought a bone with me this morning. It's not because I have a bone to pick with you. Have you heard that expression before? It means that we have some difference of opinion that's bothering me. As I was reading today's Scripture lesson about Ezekiel and the Valley of Dry Bones, I thought about how we use the imagery of bones today.

For instance have you heard anyone say, "The problem with him is that he doesn't have any backbone?" That means that he doesn't have courage, doesn't it?

Or you might hear someone say, "He's such a bone head." That probably means he's not too smart.

Or your mother might say to you, "You're such a lazy-bone." I understand that in Holland there is a holiday called Lazybones Day. Some of us are lazybones, are't we?

God showed the prophet Ezekiel a valley of Dry Bones when he wanted to help Ezekiel understand his great power. That was God's dramatic way of saying to Ezekiel, "If you have a problem, I can help you with it." That's what God is saying to you and me too. No problem is too big for God.

COUNTERCLOCKWISE WHIRLPOOLS

Scripture Lesson: Job 38:1
Objects: A plug for a sink or bath tub and a globe.

Boys and girls, in our scripture lesson God speaks to Job through a whirlwind. Have you ever seen a whirlwind? (**Let them answer.**) I've seen a whirlpool. Everytime I finish taking a bath, I pull the plug and watch the water start whirling round and round as it starts down the drain. Have you ever watched water do that? I found out something interesting about which way water turns when it goes down the drain. That's why I brought this plug with me. I could have brought my rubber ducky with me, but I would have felt kind of silly.

Did you know that if we pull a plug in a sink here in America, most of the time the water will turn to the left, that is counterclockwise, as it swirls down the drain. Try it when you get home. It will turn to the left. However, if we lived in Buenos Aires, Argentina or in Perth, Australia the water would turn to the right. That is because they are south of the equator. The swirling of the water is caused by the rotation of the earth. Did you know that at the equator the earth is turning at a rate of more than 1000 miles per hour. You and I can't even feel it, can we? But the world is turning that fast. And that is what makes the water turn leftward as it swirls out of our bath tub.

I've never seen a real whirlpool or a real whirlwind like Job did. But I still hear God speak. He speaks through the Bible. He speaks through the quietness of my own thought and through my conscience. He speaks through the people I love. God is always speaking to us — telling us what is the good and right thing to do.

TIME TO HUDDLE

Scripture Lesson: John 17:1-11
Object: A football.

Boys and girls,

I know that it is not quite football season yet. But I want you to use your imagination for a few moments. I want you to imagine that we are a football team. **(Hold the ball under your arm like a running back.)** I have received the opening kickoff and I have been tackled on the twenty yard line. What is the next thing we do? **(Give them a chance to answer.)** Pass? Run? No, before that. That's right, we make a huddle. **(Have the children make a huddle.)** We gather in a circle. We could hold hands. Some of the pro and college teams do that. Sometimes they put their arms around each other's shoulders. Some of us are embarrassed to do that. That will change in a few years. What do we do now in the huddle? That's right – we plan our next play. When we huddle like this, it also reminds us that we are teammates, doesn't it? We work together as a team.

I like to think of Sunday School and Worship as a Christian's huddle. They help us get ready for the coming week. They remind us who else is on our team. Jesus prayed that his disciples would always be a team. He didn't put it that way, but that's what he meant. That's why it is so important for us to get together in our huddle each week. Sunday School and Worship – the Christian's huddle.

GOD HAS NO FAVORITES

Scripture Lesson: I Peter 1:17-23
Object: A piece of stick candy large enough to be divided (have a stick for all the children).

Boys and girls:

I need two volunteers this morning. Let's have a girl and a boy. O.K. — you two will be fine. I have a piece of candy I would like to share with you. I hope that's all right with you. Now I don't have any way to divide this piece of candy evenly. I'll just have to break it. But wait. What if one piece is larger? (Jane), would you be upset if I gave (Bill) a larger piece than I gave you? How about you, (Bill)? Would you be upset if you got the smaller piece? Maybe you might think that I like girls more than boys.

That happens sometimes in families, doesn't it? You might think that your parents like your brother or sister more than they like you. You are probably mistaken about that, but sometimes we may feel that way. In school we may feel that our teachers have favorites. Have you ever heard of a teacher's pet?

Our Scripture lesson today tells us that God doesn't play favorites. The way the King James Version translates I Peter 1:17 is that God is no respector of persons. That simply means that God doesn't play favorites. He loves all of his children the same. It doesn't matter whether they have dark skin or white skin. It doesn't matter whether they are rich or very poor. It doesn't matter whether they live in America or Russia or China or Africa. All of God's children are important to him. That means that you are important to him — and so am I.

I wouldn't want either of you to feel that I love one of you more than the other, so I won't try to divide this piece of candy. Actually I have a piece of candy for everybody — and they are all the same size. As you take one I want you to remember that God doesn't play favorites. He loves us all the same.

106

LITTLE NANCY ETTICOAT

Scripture Lesson: John 1:1-18

Boys and girls:

There is a rhyme that is also a riddle. It goes like this:

> *"Little Nancy Etticoat*
> *In a white petticoat,*
> *And a red nose;*
> *The longer she stands*
> *The shorter she grows."*

What is little Nancy Etticoat? That's right, she's a white candle. Her "red nose" is her flame — and the longer she stands, the shorter she grows. As we come closer to Christmas, candles become very important in the church. For they symbolize one of the beautiful passages in the Bible describing the coming of Christ: "The people who sat in darkness have seen a great light . . . ."

You know what it is to stumble through the house at night when the lights are off. Living without Christ would be like that. Remember that when you see a candle light this Christmas — Christ is the light that shines through the darkness.

HOW HIGH CAN YOU CLIMB?

Scripture Lesson: Luke 1:26-38

Object: An angel and a step ladder. (If one of the children could be dressed as an angel and have one of your larger children bring in and set up a step ladder, you would really get the children's attention.)

How high can you climb? Many of you when you were very young were climbing before you were walking. Most of us like to climb. When we are very small, we like to climb stairs or climb up on chairs. As we get older we like to climb mountains. How high can you climb?

I heard about a rather foolish young man years ago who wanted to carve his name on a rock at Natural Bridge, Virginia, higher than anybody ever had before. He climbed and climbed up on some high rocks. Soon he had gone farther up the side of the steep cliff than anyone had before. There he carved his name. Then he started back down. Suddenly he realized it was much more difficult to go down the side of this mountain than it was to go up. Indeed, it would be very dangerous to start back down. Instead he decided that it would be safer to climb on top of the cliff and start down from the other side. Needless to say, people below were very relieved when he finally made it to the top.

How high can you climb? Can you climb to the top of this ladder? Of course you can. Can you climb to the top of a mountain? Some mountains you can. Can you climb to the moon? You could if you had a space ship, couldn't you? Could you climb high enough to reach God? No, no one will ever be able to climb high enough to reach God. But that's why we have this Christmas angel. The angel reminds us that we don't have to climb up to God. God has come down to us. He came to Mary through an angel. He came to all of us in the baby Jesus. We couldn't climb up to God, so he reached down to us. He became a tiny baby in a manger so that we could see Him and love Him and know that He loves us.

WHY THE HOLLY HAS RED BERRIES

Scripture Lesson: Luke 2:1-20
Object: A holly branch.

Do you know why the holly has red berries? A long time ago, so the story goes, the trees heard a rumor that if a king should walk in their shade the first tree that should recognize him would become more beautiful than all the others. Now it happened that outside the little town of Nazareth there grew a forest of big cedars, firs, and oaks, and among them one little holly tree. One day a boy came out of the town and walked through the forest. Each of the big trees thought, "He is looking at me." But the little holly tree as it watched him forgot about itself. Many times the boy walked in the forest until the big trees became so accustomed to him that they gave him no attention. But the holly tree still watched him and said to itself, "Surely if a king were to come he would not be so beautiful as this boy. He is always kind; the birds and the animals are not afraid of him. I wish he were my king; I should like to obey him."

After a time, the little boy no longer went to the forest. The holly tree missed him very much, but it thought about him and tried to be like him and to do the things it believed he would want it to do. It was kind to the birds and the animals. It spread its branches so that the birds could build their nests in them. It made little houses down among its roots for small animals. The other trees thought it was not worth noticing, but it kept sweet-tempered and did not quarrel with them.

The little boy grew to be a man and traveled about the country, telling people about God and how men might please God by loving one another. But one day wicked men took him and put a robe on him such as kings wear, and made a crown of thorny twigs and placed it on his head. Then they nailed him to a cross and over his head was placed a sign which read, "The King."

A wonderful change now came to the little holly tree growing just outside of Nazareth. Between its dark green leaves little

109

red berries began to grow until it was arrayed in a royal robe of scarlet, because, you see, it was the first of the trees to recognize the King.

Yes, it was Jesus, King of heaven and earth. To recognize him as King, to desire to obey him and to be like him, is to become beautiful — beautiful in character. It means to be arrayed like him in a robe of righteousness. Amid the hurry and the excitement, the gift-making and the gift-receiving, the good-will and the joy of the Christmas season, shall we not take time to think that it is the birthday of our King?

THE SUN OF GOD

Scripture Lesson: John 1: 6-8; 19-28
Object: A Star from a Christmas tree.

Boys and girls, this is a good time to talk about the North Pole. Why is it a good time to talk about the North Pole? That's right. Christmas is getting close and there is a lot of activity at the North Pole.

But I want to tell you something else about the North Pole. They don't have days and nights at the North Pole like we have. Winter is one long, dark night lasting for months and months. We are told that there is a custom in villages near the North Pole. The people in those villages wait patiently through those long, dark winters. No light at all for months and months. But when the time is very near for the sun to rise again, the people send messengers to the highest point to watch. As the first streaks of light break through, the messengers cry out, "Behold the sun!" The people put on their brightest clothes and they hug one another and they celebrate. The sun has finally risen after months and months of nights.

That is the way the *Bible* speaks about the birth of baby Jesus. The world was very dark with hate and evil. But then a light shone through the darkness. It was the Bethlehem star shining on a manger in a stable where the baby Jesus lay. He would be the light of the world. He would show people how to live in peace and love together. We might call him the Sun of God, s-u-n, or the Son, s-o-n of God. But He is the reason we celebrate Christmas. Like those villagers, we can sing out, "Behold the Son!"

111

LOOKING FOR A ROAD SIGN

Scripture Lesson: Matthew 24:36-44
Object: A map.

Boys and girls: (open the map.)

Have you ever been in a car and been lost? Perhaps your family was on vacation in a strange place. Maybe it was in a large city or maybe it was in the open country. But somehow you took a wrong turn. Eagerly everyone started looking for a road sign. What street is that up ahead? Where are we on the map? Maybe your father got angry. I do sometimes. Most of us do when we are worried and frustrated. But you didn't wander forever. You made it back here to church this Sunday, didn't you?

Of course, there was a time when there weren't any road signs or maps. Back then everyone was an explorer. As you travelled you might make notches on trees so you could find your way back. you might follow a river or set your course by the stars. Two thousand years ago three astrologers were searching for signs in the stars, and they saw one star that was far brighter and they followed that star 'til it led them to Bethlehem. What did they find in Bethlehem? That's right — they found a young child with his mother, Mary, and his father, Joseph. The young child was named Jesus.

The next four Sundays for us will be four Sundays of waiting and looking toward the heavens and preparing ourselves for the celebration of Christ's coming into the world. I know some of you are looking already toward the sky for Santa and his reindeer, aren't you? Let's do more than that, though. Let's look for Jesus. Let's prepare our hearts to make Him our Savior and our Lord. Let's look for His road-signs. Road-signs that lead to peace, love, and joy.

GROWING UP AND CHRISTMAS

Scripture Lesson: Luke 2:41-52
Object: A Christmas toy.

I'll bet Santa Claus was good to you this Christmas. I'll bet that for some of us this was the best Christmas ever. Of course, the meaning of Christmas changes for us as we get older. When we are very small, Christmas may mean lots of toys. As we get near the teenage years, we may start getting more clothes for Christmas and less toys. That's hard sometimes. But we ought to be proud of that, too. That means we are growing. Then when we get to be adults Santa Claus may not bring us anything at all, but Christmas is still very special to us. Part of the happiness we feel is the joy of watching you have such a good time. We adults start to understand what the Bible means when it says that it is more blessed to give than to receive.

The meaning of Christmas changes as we grow. Jesus grew, too. The Bible says he grew in wisdom and in stature, and in favor with God and man. It is a good thing to grow. Even if it does mean more clothes and less toys. God wants us to grow not only physically, but mentally. That is why school is so important. And spiritually. That is why Sunday School and church are so important — that we, too, may grow in wisdom and stature, and in favor with God and man.

THE TWELFTH DAY OF CHRISTMAS

Scripture Lesson: Matthew 2:9-10
Object: A candle.

One of the silliest songs ever written is a song about the twelve days of Christmas. Have any of you heard that song? It is a song about the gifts that someone gave his girlfriend. Did you give your girlfriend something for Christmas? You're a little bit young for that. The fellow in this song gets a little carried away. You remember on the first day of Christmas he gives his girlfriend a partridge in a pear tree. Then on the second day he gives her two calling birds. Then three turtle doves — four french hens — five golden rings — six geese a-layin' — seven swans a swimming — eight maids a milking — nine ladies dancing — ten lords a-leaping — eleven pipers piping — twelve drummers drumming. Wow! Each day for twelve days a bigger, and more extravagant gift. What a ridiculous song!

Do you know where the idea of twelve days of Christmas came from? We don't know exactly when Jesus was born. At first people celebrated his birthday on January 6, not on December 25. It was not until 300 years after Jesus' death and resurrection that people began to celebrate his birth on December 25. As more and more people celebrated December 25 as Christmas Day, January 6 — the twelfth day of Christmas — came to be celebrated as the day when the three wise men came to worship Jesus. In our Christmas plays we have the three wise men kneeling beside the shepherds in the stable. The Bible actually says that the three wise men came to a "house" where the "young child" lay. In some churches that twelfth day of Christmas is known as "Epiphany." A candle is a good symbol for Epiphany. During this season of the year we celebrate the fact that Christ is the light of the world.

So now you know where the twelve days of Christmas came from. Actually it would be great if we could have 365 days of Christmas — 365 days of peace and love and joy. We can have his light in our hearts, though. We can be a Christmas candle all year long.

"LONG AGO IN ONE'S LIFE"

Object: A clock.

Boys and Girls:

There is a song that people often sing on New Year's Eve called *"Auld Lang Syne."* It is a Scottish song, and the words *Auld Lang Syne* mean "old times" or "long ago in one's life." People sing this song as they remember their friends of the past year and years before. They sing:

> **"Should old acquaintance be forgot**
> **and never brought to mind?**
>
> Should old acquaintance be forgot
> in days of auld lang syne?"

Some of you have moved from one place to another. You've changed schools and left behind friends whom you cared about very much. You remember the good times you had together, and you cherish their friendship even though you're away from them. Some of you who are in Scouts sing another song about friends:

> **"Make new friends, but keep the old,**
> **One is silver, and the other's gold."**

And you know, that's true. Think about those friends around you right now; they are as precious to you as gold and silver aren't they?

Now would be a good time, as the old year ends and the new year begins, to remember your friends and be thankful for them.

WILL GIZZARDS MAKE US BEAUTIFUL?

Object: A chestnut or some black-eyed peas.

Boys and Girls:

Childcraft Encyclopedia tells us of some unusual foods that people eat to celebrate the New Year:

People in Japan eat a fish called **carp**. Carp are able to swim against strong currents and even leap waterfalls. So, as they eat carp, people hope that they, too, will be able to do difficult things in the coming year.

"People in Hungary eat roast pig with an apple or a four-leaf clover in its mouth, and they hope for a lucky year."

"In other lands, people eat black-eyed peas to make them strong, chestnuts to bring them good luck, or even chicken gizzards to make them beautiful during the coming year."

Of course, we know that eating carp won't insure us that we will be able to do difficult things in the coming year; and eating roast pig won't really bring us good luck, or black-eyed peas won't, by themselves, make us strong, or eating chestnuts won't bring us good luck, or eating chicken gizzards won't necessarily make us beautiful.

But there are some things that can make us strong and healthy and even lucky. Lots of good exercise, eating the right kinds of foods, studying hard in school, and letting God be our friend and our partner in everything we do.

HAPPY OLD YEAR

Scripture Lesson: Psalm 111
Object: A party hat (one also for each of the children if possible) and a broom.

I don't know about you, but I just can't wait to celebrate Happy Old Year's Day! Are you going to celebrate Old Year's Day this year? What's that? You are going to celebrate New Year's Day. They celebrated it on the last day of the year. In some parts of England men and boys used to put black soot on their faces like chimney sweeps and carry around brooms to sweep the old year out. Old Year's Day was even bigger than New Year's Day.

Of course we look forward to the New Year. But let's not forget the old year. There's something exciting about new things. We like our new toys, but let's not forget our old toys. We like making new friends, but let's not forget our old friends. As you grow up you will learn many new lessons in life. But don't forget the old.

Probably the first song you ever learned to sing was "Jesus Loves Me, This I Know." Don't ever forget that song, because it is true. Your world is filled with important people like teachers and friends — but don't take for granted those who love you the most — your parents and grandparents, aunts and uncles, etc.

Enjoy the new year, but don't forget the old. You probably won't celebrate Old Year's Day this year. You will probably just call it New Year's Eve. But never forget that some things that are old are very, very good.

APRIL FISH

Scripture Lesson: John 9:1-14
Object: Make a simple dunce hat.

Boys and girls,

Oh, excuse me (John) there's a fly on the end of your nose. Oh you don't see it? Well, April fool. If we were in France we would say April Fish. April Fool's Day is a silly holiday. It's when we play tricks on each other. Have you had a trick played on you today?

Do you know where April Fool's Day came from? I understand that long ago New Year's Day was celebrated on April 1. But some people forgot. They celebrated at the old time. So they were called April fools.

Actually, it's not good to make anyone feel foolish, is it? Sometimes we can be very cruel to each other with our jokes and our tricks. Sometimes we call people names that really hurt. Sometimes people hurt us with their jokes.

Jesus knew what it was to have people be cruel to him. They criticized him even when he was doing good. They made fun of him. They beat him and finally they crucified him. But they could not stop him from loving. Even on the cross he forgave those who had hurt him.

That's how he wants us to be. He doesn't want us to make an April fool out of anyone. He wants us to love people and to do everything we can to build them up. That's what he did.

TWO SUGGESTIONS FOR PALM SUNDAY

Scripture Lesson: Luke 22:1-23; 56
Children like to "do as well as to "see" and "hear." The objects for both of these suggestions are the children's bodies.

LIVING CROSSES

If you have lots of older children you might want to line them up horizontally and vertically to make a large "living cross." Have each of them hold their arms straight out on each side to make a cross out of their own body. As they stand in that position, remind them that the church is that group of people charged with the responsibility of reminding the world about the cross of Jesus Christ. Remind them also that each of us as individuals are "living crosses" —telling the world about Jesus' love.

PRAISING GOD WITH OUR BODIES

Using **"Doxology"** have the boys and girls reach their hands toward the ceiling and gradually lower them as they sing "Praise God from whom all blessings flow." As they come to the end of this line, have them make a bowl with their hands to receive God's blessings. Then have them hold out their arms as if they are getting ready to give someone a big hug — open them wide enough for the whole world — as they sing "Praise Him all creatures here below." Have them lift their hands slowly toward the ceiling again as they sing "Praise Him above ye heavenly hosts, Praise Father," then have them hold their arms straight out on the sides to make themselves into a cross as they sing "Son," then put their hands together in kind of a "praying hands" gesture as they raise them toward the ceiling then lower them as they sing "and Holy Ghost."

As they lower their hands, still in the "praying hands" position, have them place their hands under their chins as they bow their head and sing, "Amen."

If you will demonstrate and carefully explain each gesture, they will have a new understanding of the **"Doxology."**

SYMBOLS OF HOLY WEEK

Scripture Lesson: Matthew 26:14-27; 66
Objects: A palm branch, a communion cup, three nails.

Boys and girls,

This is a very special week for Christians. Does anybody know what this week is called? That's right, it is Holy Week. This week we celebrate the last week in Jesus' life. I brought with me three very simple but important symbols of this week.

What is this first one? That's right, it is a palm branch. That is because today is Palm Sunday. Palm Sunday celebrates the day Jesus rode into Jerusalem on a donkey and the people—particularly the boys and girls – waved palm branches and shouted, "Hosanna, blessed is he that comes in the name of the Lord."

On Monday Jesus went to the temple and drove out the money-changers and began to teach. At night he and his disciples would sleep in a secluded spot outside the city.

On Thursday night, they had a very special meal together. I have a cup here with me to symbolize that meal. We often call that meal the Last Supper. At that supper Jesus revealed that one of his disciples would betray him and that he would be crucified. Who was the disciple who betrayed Jesus? That's right, Judas.

These nails symbolize what happened on Friday. What was that? That's right. Jesus was crucified. But that's not the end of the story, is it. On the third day – the first Easter Sunday – Jesus came back to life. That is what Holy Week is about. It is that very special week leading up to the most special day of all. Next Sunday we will gather here for a great service to tell the world that Jesus who was crucified is now alive. Holy Week helps us get ready for that great day.

THE HUMBLEST OF CREATURES

Scripture Lesson: Mark 11:1-11
Object: A picture of a donkey or perhaps a rope for an imaginary rein.

Boys and girls,

There is hardly a creature more lowly thought of than the donkey. How would you like to be called a donkey? Donkeys are like Rodney Dangerfield, aren't they? They get no respect.

Isn't it interesting then that the greatest man who ever lived would choose a donkey to ride on when he rode into Jerusalem. If you were going to lead a parade in our town, would you choose a nice horse or a lowly donkey? Most of us would choose the horse.

Even before Jesus was born, a donkey was important in in his story. Do you remember why? That's right. Mary rode a donkey to Bethlehem before Jesus was born.

So we have the lowliest of creatures chosen to play an important role in the story of the King of Kings. You know, that was no accident. There was one kind of people whom Jesus didn't like − it was people who were kind of stuck up. You know what I am talking about? People who went around with their nose in the air saying, "I've got nicer clothes than you. My family lives in a better subdivision than yours. Let's not associate with her. Her family doesn't have any money." Jesus liked and forgave just about everybody. The only group Jesus couldn't stand were snobs − whether they were snobs because of their religion or because of their money.

Snobs can't really be what Jesus wants his disciples to be because they break the second most important commandment. They do not love others. They only love themselves. So remember the lowly donkey the next time you see somebody act like a snob. You can't be a snob and be a follower of Jesus.

"HOORAY FOR JESUS"

Scripture Lesson: Luke 19:28-40
Object: A pom-pom.

Not very many people in America live in a place where they can go out and cut a palm branch to wave on Palm Sunday, can they, boys and girls? Depending on what area of the country we live in we might be able to get a limb of an oak, or a pine, or a dogwood or even a giant redwood. But generally we don't wave pine branches or dogwood branches or even palm branches when we have a parade. That's why I have this pom-pom with me.

Now we normally don't have pom-poms in church on Sunday morning, do we? Where would you normally find a pom-pom? **(Let them respond)** That's right, at a ball game or maybe at a parade. How do we use a pom-pom? Do we use it to dust with? **(make a dusting motion.)** Or perhaps we wear it on our head? **(Place it on your head.)** What do we do with a pom-pom? We wave it don't we? And we yell "Hooray for our team!" That is the purpose of a pom-pom.

No, we normally don't have pom-poms in church on Sunday morning. And yet, I felt that maybe this pom-pom would help us best of all catch the spirit of Palm Sunday — the day those boys and girls two-thousand years ago shook their pom-pom and yelled, "Hooray for Jesus!" That's not exactly how they did it, is it? They waved palm branches and shouted "Hosanna!" That's the way they did it back then. But if it were today, I believe they would shake pom-poms and shout, "Hooray for Jesus!" In fact, let's try that right now. All together **(Build them to a crescendo, perhaps several times.)** "Hooray for Jesus!" **(Be sure to shake the pom-pom joyously.)**

RESCUE THE PERISHING

Scripture Lesson: Luke 15
Object: A symbol of the Red Cross, United Way, or a special mission program in your own church.

Boys and girls,

William Saroyan has written many outstanding stories for young people. One of his stories is entitled, **"The Rescue of the Perishing."** It is about a 12 year old boy who has a very loving heart. There is a great flood in his town. He volunteers to help the men as they try to contain the flood's damage. He worked just as hard as any of the adult men. Later as he was walking home from the library he comes upon a chicken hiding under a car and also a small dog hiding under another car. They had obviously gotten lost in the storm. At first the chicken and the dog are both afraid of him. Soon, however, he wins their trust and he takes them home with him.

Now Jesus did not tell stories about lost chickens and lost dogs, but he did tell stories about lost sheep and lost coins and even a lost boy. Jesus loved stories like that. If Jesus had read William Saroyan's story, he would have said that God is like that boy who went to help people in the flood. God cares about a chicken and a small dog hiding under automobiles. God wants to help wherever there is trouble.

You know, I believe that there is something in every boy and girl's heart that wants to help others. We sometimes act selfishly as if we don't care. But I believe we do care. How are some ways that we show people we care about them? (**Let them suggest some ways. Then use this time to say to the adults, "I believe every one of our adults, your mothers and fathers, want to help others too. Here is one way all of us can help. Then lift up some particular project.**)

HE IS NOT HERE
4/12/98 *(EASTER SUNDAY)*

Scripture Lesson: Mark 16:1-8
Object: From a piece of cardboard make a simple tombstone. Write on it "He is not here; He is risen." Do not show it to the children until the end.

Boys and girls:

It is very interesting sometimes to go through old cemeteries and read the tombstones. Often, you can read about persons who lived hundreds of years ago. Sometimes people used to have sayings – called epitaphs – inscribed on their tombstone. Some of these are quite silly. Here is an epitaph off one grave.* See if you can figure out what happened to this person:

In Memory of
Anna Hopewell
Here lies the body of Anna
Done to death by a banana
It wasn't the fruit that laid her low
But the skin of the thing that made her go.

What do you suppose happened to Anna? That's right. She slipped on a banana peel.

Now I'm not an artist. But on this piece of cardboard, I have made a tombstone for Jesus. Jesus has been dead for 2,000 years, so I thought I would make a tombstone for his grave. And I have written an epitaph to go on that tombstone. Now this epitaph isn't a funny one. It is serious. What do you think I wrote on Jesus' tombstone? What are some of the things I could have written: "He was crucified. He was the Son of God. He died for me." Those might be some of the things. Here is what I wrote though on Jesus' tombstone: "He is not here, He is risen." That's what Easter is all about, isn't it. Jesus Christ is alive.

*from *The People's Almanac No. 2*, David Wallechinsky and Iriving Wallace, Editors.

QUIT BEING A CATERPILLAR

Scripture Lesson: Ecclesiastes 3:11
Object: A caterpillar (live in a jar if possible; if not, then perhaps a picture).

When we see this ugly old caterpillar, boys and girls, it is hard for us to believe that someday it will be a beautiful — what? Butterfly, of course. This ugly old caterpillar will spin himself — or herself, I don't know which — into a beautiful — what? Cocoon, of course. It will spend some time in the cocoon and then come out as a beautiful, graceful butterfly. Right now this caterpillar can only crawl across the ground, but one day he will be able to do what? That's right, he will be able to fly up in the sky.

For a lot of people the caterpillar is the best example there is of life after death. When we die, according to the Bible, God gives us a new and more beautiful body than the one we have on the earth.

This old caterpillar also reminds me of another fact, though. We don't have to die for God to make us more beautiful. He can make us into beautiful people right now. In the book of Ecclesiastes we read, "He hath made everything beautiful in its time . . . . " God can help us love everyone more — our friends, our parents, our brothers and sisters. A person filled with God's love is always more beautiful.

This ugly old caterpillar doesn't have to stay a caterpillar forever. Neither do we. We can be beautiful people if we give Him our hearts and love one another more.

GOD OF THE LIVING

Scripture Lesson: Job 19:23-27a;
Luke 20:27-38

Object: A piece of black poster paper on the back of which you have glued several pieces of colored poster paper.

Boys and girls:

When you see black, what do you think of? (**Hold up the black piece of paper.**) Black is not a very happy color, is it? A black day is not a happy day. Black is usually thought of as the color of death. We don't talk much about death in our children's talks, but it is a very important matter in our daily lives. Some of you have had a pet who has died, haven't you? And that was a very sad day. Some of you have lost a grandmother or grandfather whom you loved very much, and oh, how it hurt. Some of you might have lost a brother or sister or mother or father. Nothing makes us sadder than the death of someone we love − until we read the words of Jesus: "God is not the God of the dead but of the living. . . . " Jesus was saying that there is a power that is greater than death. It is the power of God's love. That love is so strong that God can give a person who is dead new life. The person we love is not gone from us forever. He or she is with God. Therefore, we don't have to wear black and be sad. (**Turn the paper around to show bright colors.**) God is the God of the living. The person we love is with God. God will love him and take care of him forever.

IMMORTALITY

Scripture Lesson: II Corinthians 5:1-10
Object: A calendar.

Boys and girls:

Do you know the story of Solomon Grundy?

> Solomon Grundy,
> Born on Monday,
> Christened on Tuesday,
> Married on Wednesday,
> Took ill on Thursday,
> Worse on Friday,
> Died on Saturday,
> Buried on Sunday,
> This is the end
> Of Solomon Grundy.

That is the way the nursery rhyme goes. But the last two lines are wrong. "This is the end of Solomon Grundy," says the poem. But that is not what the Bible tells us. The Bible tells us that dying is not the end of things at all. When we die, we go to live with God. Somebody ought to rewrite the last lines like this:

> Died on Saturday,
> Buried on Sunday,
> And now God has
> Solomon Grundy.

MY CUP OVERFLOWS

Scripture Lesson: Psalm 23; Galatians 1:11-24
Object: A can of Tab (or some other highly carbonated soft drink) and a
small cup and bowl.

Boys and girls, do you remember the twenty-third Psalm? How does it begin? That's right, "The Lord is my shepherd. . . " Can someone recite the whole Psalm? **(If you have a volunteer, have them begin, or have someone read the Psalm. When they come to the place where it says, "my cup overflows . . . " pour the Tab into the cup until the foam overflows.)** My cup over-flows. **(Resume pouring the Tab until not only the foam but the drink itself begins to overflow.)** God gives us His Spirit to the point that we overflow with happiness and love and joy. The early Christians knew about that overflow after the day of Pentecost when the Holy Spirit came upon them. They were so happy that some people thought they were drunk. The Holy Spirit filled them so full that they had to tell others. Through them the Spirit overflowed into others. St. Paul didn't experience that overflow until a little later, but it changed his whole life.

Did you notice though when we poured the drink into the cup there were two kinds of overflow? The first time we only poured a little of the drink into the cup, didn't we? And what happened? That's right, the foam overflowed. That happens in worship sometimes. It makes us very happy. It may even give us a "bubbly" kind of feeling. But the foam or the fizz doesn't last long, does it? Sometimes that little bit of Spirit we got on Sunday morning just doesn't make it 'til Monday. The second time we poured the drink, the drink itself overflowed – not just the foam or fizz. That's the kind of overflow that David was talking about in this Psalm – when our lives are so filled with His Spirit to the point that other people can share in the overflow.

SYMBOLS OF THE SPIRIT

Scripture Lesson: Acts 2:1-21
Objects: A dove (a picture or drawing will do) and a match. (If you have denominational symbols featuring a dove or a flame, they would be excellent to use here.)

Boys and girls,

This is the day of Pentecost — fifty days after Easter — when we celebrate the coming of the Holy Spirit upon the church 2,000 years ago. Nobody knows what the Holy Spirit looks like because the Holy Spirit is part of God and no one has ever seen God, but there are three symbols for the Holy Spirit in the Bible.

I have a drawing here of a dove. Does anybody know why the dove is a symbol of the Holy Spirit? It comes from a story about Jesus. After his baptism the Bible tells us that the Holy Spirit came upon him in the form of a dove. So the dove is a symbol of the Holy Spirit.

Now I want you to see two symbols at once. I'm going to light this match. The flame is one symbol. Now watch. **(Blow out the flame.)** The third symbol you can't see either. It is my breath or the wind.

Let's think, first of all, about the flame. That comes from today's reading of the Bible. When the Holy Spirit came upon the disciples, the Bible says that there were flames of fire above the heads of the disciples. So the flame became a symbol for the Holy Spirit.

It was Jesus, though, that told us that the Spirit was like the wind. You can't see the wind, can you? You can't control the wind. But a mighty wind can pick up a house and move it. Jesus said the Holy Spirit of God is like that. You can't see it, but when the Spirit moves, people's lives are changed.

What are the three symbols for the Holy Spirit? That's right. A dove, a flame, and the wind.

ONE OUT OF TEN

Scripture Lesson: Luke 17:11-19
Objects: Ten dimes, ten seeds

Suppose, boys and girls, you had ten dimes. How much does that make? That's right. Ten dimes make a dollar. Suppose you had ten dimes and you lost nine of them on the way to the store. Maybe you had a tiny hole in your pocket just big enough to let one dime at a time slip through. When you got to the store, you had only one dime left. How would you feel?

Suppose you planted a garden. Suppose you had ten seeds to plant in that garden. You might very carefully hoe the garden and then plant the seeds, water them every day, pull out weeds that might threaten them. But suppose after all of your care, only one of those seeds actually grew into a plant. That wouldn't make much of a garden, would it?

Perhaps we can appreciate the way Jesus felt then. Ten men came to him who had the terrible disease of leprosy. He sent them to the temple and told them that they would be healed. They were healed. All ten of them were now whole. But only one took the time to come back to Jesus to say "thank you." Only one out of ten! Obviously their bodies were healed but not their souls. We are never the kind of people we ought to be until we learn to say thank you. Thank you to God. Thank you to our parents. Thank you to our friends when they've done something helpful for us. Only one out of ten came back to give thanks. Let's hope that you and I do better than that.

GOD EVEN LOOKS AFTER TURKEYS

Scripture Lesson: Matthew 10:26-33
Object: A bird's feather or a picture of a turkey.

Boys and girls,

Has anyone ever called you a turkey? I hope not. What does it mean to call somebody a turkey? **(Let them answer.)** It means you're stupid, a klutz, doesn't it? I hope nobody calls you a turkey, and I hope you never call anybody else a turkey. We don't want anybody to feel put down, do we?

I was reading somewhere about baby turkeys. Did you know that a baby turkey has to be taught to eat or it will starve. Turkeys aren't too bright, are they? In fact, a lot of baby turkeys drown during rainstorms because they tend to look up into the rain with their mouths open. That's a sad thing to think about, but it shows you how slow turkeys are.

In our Scripture lesson, Jesus tells us that God watches over the little sparrows in the sky. Not one of them falls without God knowing about it. Then he goes on to say that we are worth a lot more than sparrows, so think how concerned God is about us! That's a beautiful thought, isn't it?

Of course we could substitute turkeys for sparrows in the Scripture lesson, couldn't we? God watches over little turkeys and cares about them even though they're not the brightest of birds. That helps me because sometimes I feel like a turkey. Do you ever feel like a turkey? Sometimes I do stupid things. Everybody does. We might even say to ourselves, "You turkey!" Then we might remind ourselves that God loves us even when we are turkeys — even when we've done something stupid and gotten ouselves in an awful mess. God still loves us even when we act like turkeys.

HIS FATHER'S SON

Scripture Lesson: 1 Samuel 16:1-5

Wonder crept across his face as he watched his father barter with the shop-keeper. His large brown eyes shown with the realization that one day he would be expected to bring the family's wool into market. He listened intently. What a shrewd bargainer his father was. How resolute he could be when he stated the lowest price he would accept. Would the shop-keeper raise his offer? The shop-keeper grumbled unhappily. "It's a bad year," he complained bitterly, "not enough rain. How can I sell these skins and make a fair profit if you want such an unreasonable price? These are hard times." David's father started for the door. "Wait just a minute. Hold on there," the shop-keeper muttered softly, "I didn't say I wouldn't pay your price." Then he broke suddenly into a smile. "You're a hard man, Jesse. You always seem to know just how much to ask. But it's fine wool. I'll find a way to keep from losing my shirt on it." David's father gave a hard laugh, "I'm sure you will. If I know you, you'll charge some unsuspecting shopper twice what you paid me — and you'll complain that he's stealing you blind." And he laughed harder. David loved to hear his father laugh. He was happy to see the shop keeper smile too. Just a few moments ago they had seemed so serious. He did not like to see people angry at one another. He did not like to be angry himself. "Why can't they disagree without getting angry? The shop-keeper was writing out a bill of sale. "Any trouble with wolves attacking your sheep this year, Jesse?" David's father's eyes grew suddenly serious. "We lost one lamb last week, and three more within the past month." Then he suddenly smiled and patted David on the shoulder, "But no more, my friend. Today I'm taking young David here out to the mountain pastures. It's time he learned to be a shepherd like his father. I doubt that any wolves will bother the flock if they know he's on guard." David's young tan face showed the slightest signs of embarrassment. He knew his father was teasing, but he did not mind. One day he would stand guard with his fathers flock. He would drive the wolves and bears from the lambs. Already he could use his sling almost as deftly as his older brother. Soon he would be taller and stronger. And suddenly he felt very proud. Proud of his growing body and proud to be Jesse's son. Yes, one day young David would be entrusted to guard his father's flock.

A SURPRISE FOR DAVID

Scripture Lesson: I Samuel 16:5-13

One day David's father Jesse got an unexpected invitation. It was from the priest Samuel. Samuel was a great priest in Israel — a man who was very close to God. In fact, God had spoken to him just recently and had told him that He had chosen a new king for the nation.

King Saul was the king at that time, but King Saul was a disappointment to God, and so God decided he would have to be replaced. God told Samuel to send for David's father Jesse and invite him to come to a special sacrificial feast. "For, " said, the Lord, "I have provided for Myself a king among his sons." Samuel did as the Lord instructed him. He went to Bethlehem which was David's home and invited Jesse and his sons to a sacrificial feast. When Jesse's oldest son came forward, a tall, handsome young man, Samuel thought to himself this must be the one that the Lord had chosen. But the Lord said, "No." "Look not on his appearance or at the height of his stature, for I have rejected him; for the Lord sees not as man sees; for man looks on the outward appearance, but the Lord looks on the heart." (I Samuel 16:7). Don't we sometimes make the same mistake. We judge people by what they look like, how they dress or what kind of house they live in, but God looks at what people are on the inside.

Six more of Jesse's sons were brought forward to Samuel, but the Lord rejected each of these as well. "Have you no other sons?" Samuel asked Jessee. Jesse replied that he did have one more younger boy, who was out guarding the sheep. "Bring him to me, " Samuel said. It was David. The Scripture describes young David like this: he has "reddish hair, fair skin, beautiful eyes and was fine looking." He didn't look much like a warrior though — much less like a king. He wasn't very big as we will see later. But the Lord told Samuel to anoint David. He was to be the new king of Israel. God saw something in David that nobody else saw — something that would one day make him a great king. God sees some great things in you

134

You may not see them. Your best friends may not see them. But God does. And if you give Him the best you that's possible, he will take you and help you do wonderful things. There is a new person inside of us just waiting to be born. It is the "us" we can be with God's help.

DAVID, THE SONGWRITER

Scripture Lesson: I Samuel 16:14-23

It seemed like only yesterday when his father had first taken him out to the mountain grazing lands. How quickly the years had passed. He was a teenager now. For several weeks he had been guarding his father's flock alone — often late into the evening. At first it was a grand adventure. He would listen intently for the sound of an approaching menace to his father's sheep. He dreamed of what he would do if a wolf or bear had tried to capture one of the lambs. He would rely upon his trusty sling. He was a deadly shot. He could hit the small sycamore tree next to the spring nearly every time. He only wished that the tree would move so that it would seem more like a wolf. Sometimes he would use his sling on the run to make his target more elusive. And if his sling should somehow fail him there was always his trusty staff. He swung it at the tree. Already it showed the marks of his many other encounters with wild beasts. How the wood stung his hands as he brought a crashing blow to the side of his fierce foe. Perspiration rolled in great drops down the side of his handsome face. "It's no good," he thought, "It's not the same. It's just a tree." He was tired now. He sat beside the sycamore. The hours passed slowly now. He reached over and picked up his lyre Music always helped the time to pass. Sometimes he sang a song he had heard in the marketplace. And there were those haunting chants from the temple. He could close his eyes and see the robed figures of men singing praise to God. There was something about the beauty of their music that caused cold chills on David's spine. "Someday I will sing in the temple, too," he thought to himself. "I will sing God's praise with reverence and beauty." And he strummed softly on his lyre as he tried to recall the chants of the temple.

Mostly, though, David made up his own songs. He sang about the trees and the clouds. He sang about his life as a shepherd. And he sang about his own feelings. And he sang about God. God was very real to David. He did not know what God looked like, but somehow he knew God loved him. He knew God was his friend. And that made him feel very strong. "God is with me," he thought to himself. "He is with me when the sun shines. And he is with me when the lightening flashes and the wind blows hard against my father's tent." And David began to sing — a song about God.

AN HONOR FOR DAVID

Scripture Lesson: I Samuel 16:14-23

We have already noted that David was a fine musician. He not only sang, he also wrote his own songs and accompanied himself on an instrument of that day called a lyre. Have you ever seen a harp? A lyre is something like a small harp. David practiced playing his lyre everyday. That's what you have to do if you want to learn to play a musical instrument really well. David became such a fine musician and had such a nice voice that others began to notice his talent. He became quite popular with the other young people in town. The would often ask him to play and sing for them.

His fame spread even into King Saul's palace. The king had disobeyed God and now was feeling very troubled. He was having trouble sleeping at night and he felt awful all day. He thought that perhaps some beautiful music would soothe his troubled mind. But he wasn't as lucky as you are. He couldn't turn on the radio or play a record on the stereo. They didn't have things like that back then. When they wanted music, they either had to play it themselves or they had to find someone who could play for them. One of the young men in King Saul's court remembered the talented young shepherd musician of Bethlehem. "I know of a young man who plays the most beautiful music you have ever heard. Let me send for him. I am sure his music will please you." With the king's permission he sent for David. David must have been very frightened when he first played for King Saul — but it didn't show. Indeed, he played and sang so well that King Saul asked him to stay on there in the palace and become Saul's armor-bearer. That was a big honor for David. It's the kind of honor that comes to young people who work hard at the right things. The people who usually do the best are sometimes not the ones who are the smartest or the most talented. Sometimes the honors come to the people who are faithful at practicing every day — people who studied every night. Do you try to do each thing you do really well? If you do, you will probably get some special honors too.

DAVID ACCEPTS A CHALLENGE

Scripture Lesson: I Samuel 17:1-40

One of the most famous characters in the Bible is a giant named "Goliath." He was an enormous man. The Bible tells us that he had a helmet of bronze upon his head, and he was armed with a coat of mail. He had greaves of bronze upon his legs and a javelin of bronze slung between his shoulders. He carried an enormous spear. He was a fierce and frightening spectacle to behold.

His nation was an enemy of David's people. In fact, the armies of the two nations were facing each other as our story begins. Goliath steps forward and issues a challenge to the people of Israel. "Choose a man for yourselves, and let him come down to me. If he is able to fight me and kill me, then we will be your servants; but if I prevail against him and kill him, then you shall be our servants and serve us."

The Bible says that the army of David's people were afraid when they heard these words. No one wanted to face this ferocious warrior. It would be as frightening as if one of us would get into a fight with a Miami Dolphin linebacker. No one would volunteer.

Young David just happened to come down from the hills where he was watching his father's sheep to the camp of the Israeli Army soon after Goliath had issued his challenge. He was bringing some food for his brothers when Goliath stepped out from the Army of the Philistines and issued his challenge once more. David was amazed that no one in his own people's army was brave enough to accept Goliath's challenge. "I will go face the giant," he said. His older brother made fun of him. Even King Saul tried to discourage him. After all, David was just a young boy and Goliath, besides being a giant of a man, was an experienced warrior. Not only was David young but he was also small — we will talk more about that next time. What chance did David have?

David was a brave young man, was he not? Have you done something brave lately? Did you know that sometimes it is just as difficult to do or say something that your friends don't like as it is to face a giant? Suppose there is a boy or girl at school whom other people don't like. Perhaps they even make fun of that boy or girl. It takes a brave young person to be a friend to someone whom everyone else dislikes. Do you have what it takes? I hope you are just as brave as David when you fight your giants.

DAVID, THE GIANT

Scripture Lesson: I Samuel 17:38-39

There are all kinds of giants in the world. We have already noted that Goliath was a giant man. He was a giant in size. But there are all kinds of giants. A person can be a giant intellectually. He can read a lot or study a lot and learn so much that his "mental" size is enormous. Or a person can do battle. "What am I," Goliath bellowed, "a dog — that you send a boy with sticks and rocks out to meet me?" The very idea made Goliath furious. Was the army of Israel making fun of him? Why the boy did not even have any armor on. Goliath snorted and snarled and he started to tell David what he was going to do to him. He was going to tear David to pieces just to show him how angry he was.

David was frightened. David was brave as we all know. But just because people are brave does not mean that they are not frightened. Bravery means simply that we do not let our fear defeat us. David was frightened as he looked at this giant facing him, but he was determined that he would not let his fear defeat him. He spoke back to Goliath trying to sound as strong and brave as he could: "You come at me with sword and spear, but I come at you in the name of the Lord of hosts. . . ."

David was remembering those times when he guarded his father's sheep and a lion or a bear would try to steal one of the sheep. Even though David was a small boy he went after the wild animal with his slingshot and drove it off. Each time after the animal had left or been killed David would thank God for helping him to be brave and strong and for helping him be accurate with his sling. If God was with him when he fought the wild animal, then surely he would be with him as he faced Goliath. Knowing that God was with him helped him be brave and strong.

God can help you face your giants too. Oh, you may never face anybody as big as Goliath. But sometimes our problems at home and school can seem like giants. God can help us face them, and together with him we can be victorious over them.

DAVID GIVES THANKS

Scripture Lesson: I Samuel 17: 50-54

Last week we saw David go out to face Goliath. We all know what happened. David twirled his sling and Goliath fell to the ground dead. The Bible does not say what David did next — but I bet I know. I bet that David went off by himself and gave thanks to God. David knew where his help came from. He knew that it was God who gave him life and health and strength and victory over his enemies.

Do you know how I know that David gave thanks to God? It is because he wrote many of his prayers of thanksgiving in the form of songs and poetry. And we can find those songs and poems in the book of Psalms.

"The Lord is my Shepherd . . . " David wrote on one occasion. "I will lift up mine eyes unto the hills from whence cometh my help," he wrote on another. "My help cometh from the Lord." When good things happen to you, do you remember to give thanks?

You are so blessed. You have plenty of food to eat, nice clothes to wear, warm houses to go home to. Do you remember to give thanks? David did. That was part of why he was so great. He remembered that it was God who had helped him defeat his giants.

LET ME BE THE CAPTAIN

Scripture: Mark 10: 35-45

Object: A blank piece of paper and a pencil.

Boys and girls,

Our object for today is simply this blank piece of paper. A blank piece of paper is not worth much--about 1/2 cent--but it could represent a great honor to you. Suppose this morning I tore this paper into many pieces *(tear the paper)* and gave each of you a piece, and asked you to write a name on that piece of paper--the name of the person you think ought to be president of our group. Then that piece of paper would be very important because it would be a ballot, wouldn't it? Now suppose the group voted for president and you were chosen. That would be a great honor, wouldn't it? It is quite an honor to be chosen as president or as captain of a team. However, suppose with that honor would come lots of hard work and responsibility. You might not be so eager to be president or captain, might you?

Jesus' disciples, James and John, wanted the honor of sitting at his right hand and his left. Jesus questioned whether they really wanted that much responsiblity.

Some of you may be elected president of your Sunday School class or of our youth group some day. As an adult you may even be elected to the highest office in our church. That would be a great honor but also a great responsibility.

We're proud of all of the officers of our church. Maybe one of your parents is an officer in our church. If so, you can be very proud. It is good to seek to be a leader in the church. It is even better to live up to your responsibilities in the church.

YOU ARE SO IMPORTANT

Scripture: Mark 10: 2-16

Object: A pocket calculator.

Boys and girls,

You are so important to God. Today's lesson from the Bible is about the time some parents tried to bring their children to Jesus so he could touch them and Jesus' disciples tried to keep them away. After all, Jesus was a very busy man—healing people and teaching. The disciples thought Jesus was much too busy to bother with little children. Boy, were they wrong. Jesus was angry when he found out the disciples were pushing away the children. *"Let the children come to me,"* said Jesus. *"Do not forbid them for to such belongs the Kingdom of God."*

You are very important to Jesus. For one thing, he sees all the good things you are going to be able to accomplish someday. That is why he gave you a brain. I was reading about our brains this week. What do you do with your brain? That's right, you think, you dream, you hope. Do you know how wonderful your brain is?

All of you know what computers are, don't you? Some of you may have small computers at home. This calculator is a very small, simple computer. A computer tries to do some of the things our brain does, doesn't it? Sometimes we hear of computers that can store millions of bits of information. Did you know that the little 10 ounce computer in your head can store trillions of bits of information? One scientist said if they built a computer big enough to store as much as the average brain it would cost 3 billion dollars.

And yet you were born with that computer right in your head. It is a free gift from God. He has entrusted it to you. All he asks of you is to go to school, study hard, and let your brain grow. Then use it to make the world a better place. Doesn't that make you feel important? It ought to. You are a unique creation of God. You are very special to Him.

LEARNING TO SHARE

Scripture: Mark 10: 17-27   10/15/00 only Awards

Object: A piece of fruit for each of the children.

Boys and girls,

There was a beautiful poem written many years ago called, *"The House by the Side of the Road."* I don't have a copy of that poem with me, but I would like to tell you the story behind the poem.

One day the author of that poem was traveling through New England. He came upon a small house at the top of a steep hill. The house was very humble and was badly in need of paint. The house was very humble and was badly in need of paint.

In front of the house was a crudely painted sign that said, "Come on in for a cool drink." The author followed a short path to a spring of ice-cold water. Nearby was a gourd dipper, so the author helped himself, for he was very thirsty. Then he noticed a basket of beautiful apples. Next to them was a sign that said, "Help yourself." The author took one of the apples and it was delicious.

He was intrigued. Who had put up the signs and where did the apples come from? He went to the little unpainted house and found there an elderly couple. Yes, the water and the fruit were their doing. But, why, he asked? The couple explained. They had never had any children. And they had never had very much money. But they had always wanted to be able to share with other people. So they shared the two things they had plentty of–the cool, fresh water and the apples off their fruit trees. They didn't have much, but you don't have to have a lot to share with others.

Learning to share is the most beautiful thing in the world. That is what life is all about. But some people never learn that. They don't know why they are unhappy, but they have become misers without even knowing it.

I wanted to share a piece of fruit with each of you today to remind you of this beautiful couple who shared what they had. And to remind you that sharing began with God who shared this beautiful world with us.

145

USE YOUR HEAD

Scripture Lesson: Ephesians 5: 15

Object: A full length pencil for each child and a tall adult volunteer from the congregation (called Mr. Jones, in this example).

Boys and girls,

I need for each of you to take a pencil. I will explain what you will be doing with it in a moment. While you are taking a pencil, I want Mr. Jones to come up front for just a moment. I chose Mr. Jones because he is just about the tallest man in our church. I want all of you to look at Mr. Jones. Now which is taller--the pencil you are holding or Mr. Jones? *(Let them answer.)*

Of course, that is a ridiculous question. Mr. Jones is much taller. But I want you to try an experiment for me. I want you to take your pencil and hold it standing straight up about 12 inches in front of one of your eyes. *(Demonstrate.)* I want you to close your other eye. Now which is taller? If you have the pencil close enough to your eye, it will look bigger than Mr. Jones. It looks that way but you know Mr. Jones is bigger. Your brain tells you that your eye is just playing a trick on you.

What would we do without a brain? God has give us such wonderful minds. I can't imagine why anybody would ever do anything that might mess up their minds, can you? Of course not. That is why I can't imagine any young person in this church ever messing with drugs, can you? I hope not. It's bad enough to see people not taking care of their bodies. Our minds, though, are even much more important than our bodies.

Your mind is a gift from God. He wants us to grow and think and learn. He want us to use our minds to make a better world for ourselves and for others.

LESSON FROM A YO-YO

Scripture Lessson: Ephesians 5: 21-31

Object: A Yo-yo. (Have some fun; practice up and do some tricks while talking.)

Boys and girls,

I probably should have given today's lesson a different title. I hope you realize that this is the yo-yo and not the person holding it. All of you have probably played with a yo-yo before. The most important trick to get a yo-yo to do is to make it "sleep" – that is, make it stay down and spin as long as you can before you yank it up. I understand that there is a man who is trying very, very hard to build a better yo-yo. The problem he has had difficulty solving is that of friction. You see, under ideal conditions a yo-yo should spin in the sleep position almost forever, but as the string rubs against the wood or the plastic or whatever the yo-yo is made of, the yo-yo spins more and more slowly. That is friction–when two bodies rub against each other.

We've talked about friction before. Friction also happens between people. Sometimes we say, "You rub me the wrong way." That's friction. Particularly in our families do we sometimes have friction. We love each other, but we get into each other's way.

God wants us all to have happy families. He wants to help us be loving, forgiving, patient and kind with one another. I understand they are having a hard time building a yo-yo with less friction. We understand, don't we? We know how much we need God's help in solving the friction in our own house.

THE SOURCE OF OUR BLESSINGS

Scripture: Mark 10: 46-52

Object: An ear of corn if one is available (a can of corn if not).

Boys and girls,

I heard about a young fellow who lived on a farm. His favorite food was corn on the cob. His father told him one day that it took 25 gallons of water to grow just one ear of corn. Can you imagine that? Twenty-five gallon jugs of water just to grow one ear of corn. The young fellow started thinking. If there were 4 ears of corn on each stalk, it would take how many gallons of water for just one stalk? That's right, it would take 100 gallons for just one stalk. Then the boy thought of the hundreds of stalks in his father's field. It made him dizzy to think of all the thousands of gallons of water he would have to carry out to the field just to water their harvest of corn.

Of course, the boy didn't have to carry all that water to the corn, did he? God provides us with rain. He provided hundreds of gallons for each stalk of corn—at least in most parts of our country.

That is just one of the blessings God pours out on us. Our story from the Bible is about a blind man named Bartimaeus. He asked for Jesus' help and Jesus restored his sight. Bartimaeus was so happy and so thankful that he became a follower of Jesus.

We all received so many blessings from God. We already have good eyes and strong bodies, and sunshine and rain, and lots of food to eat and people who love us. Wouldn't it be great if we were as happy and as grateful as Bartimaeus? Wouldn't it be great if we became better followers of Jesus, too?

ROLL OUT THE RED CARPET

Scripture Lesson: John 6: 24-35

Object: Roll of Red Construction Paper to be an imaginary red carpet.

Boys and girls,

I want to roll out the red carpet for you this morning. *(Unroll the paper.)* What does it mean to roll out the red carpet? That is an expression we use to mean that we want to give somebody a royal welcome. When they roll out the red carpet for you, it means you are very special, very important. Whenever kings and queens are visiting another country, their hosts will roll out a red carpet to show that they are important and they are very welcome.

Since you are very important to me and to our church I want to roll out the red carpet for you. Of course, this is a make believe carpet, but the idea is still the same.

I understand that the custom of rolling out the red carpet for kings and queens started hundreds of years ago. In many places back then they didn't have nicely paved roads and concrete sidewalks like we do now. And they certainly didn't want their kings and queens to get their feet muddy. So they rolled out a special red carpet for them to walk on.

I wish that when Jesus first came into our world, people would have treated him like someone very special. Instead, they treated him like a criminal and crucified him on a cross. But we don't have to make the same mistake. We can roll out a red carpet and make him very welcome into our hearts, can't we?

Jesus is very special to us, isn't he? So let's pretend that our make believe red carpet is for him as well as for each of you–after all, he is the King of Kings.

CATCHING FLIES

Scripture Lesson: Ephesians 4: 30—5-2

Objects: A jar of honey and a bottle of vinegar.

Boys and girls,

The title of today's lesson is "Catching Flies." I don't know if any of you are interested in catching flies or not. If you are a softball or baseball player in the outfield, you've caught flies–fly balls, that is. Most of us are not interested in catching the other kind of flies.

Nevertheless, there is an old expression that goes like this: You can catch more flies with honey than with vinegar. Suppose I poured some honey here at the front of the sanctuary and also some vinegar. Which do you think that the flies would enjoy the most? I think they would prefer the honey, too. Why? That's right, the honey's sweeter.

Of course, this old saying really hasn't got anything to do with catching flies. It is about getting along with people. If you want to have friends it is much better to be like honey than like vinegar, isn't it?

Why are some people like vinegar–all sour and unfriendly and angry? Maybe it's because they don't know how much God loves them. Maybe they need us to show them that we care about them. Then they will learn how much God loves them.

Let's not spread vinegar around. Let's spread honey. Let's show the world how friendly, how pleasant, how happy the love of God can make everybody.